Captain Bligh's
PORTABLE
NIGHTMARE

*John Toohey is a photographer, historian,
documentary maker and journalist.
He lives in Perth, Australia.*

Engraved by J. Condé.

CAPT. BLIGH.

Captain Bligh's
PORTABLE
NIGHTMARE

John Toohey

FOURTH ESTATE • *London*

This paperback edition first published in 2000
First published in Great Britain in 1999 by
Fourth Estate Limited
6 Salem Road
London W2 4BU

1 3 5 7 9 10 8 6 4 2

John Fryer and *A copy of the Draught from which the Bounty's
Launch was built* reproduced from the Image Library,
State Library of New South Wales.
Maps at the start of Chapters 1, 3 & 5
drawn by Alex Snellgrove

A catalogue record for this book is available from the
British Library.

ISBN 1-84115-078-9

Typeset by MATS, Southend-on-Sea, Essex

Printed in Great Britain by Clays Ltd, St. Ives plc

Contents

Illustrations

Continue O Lord we beseech thee,
through the mediation of our blessed Saviour Jesus Christ,
this thy goodness towards us,
—strengthen my mind & guide our steps—Grant unto
us health and strength to continue our Voyage,
& so bless our miserable morsel of Bread,
that it may be sufficient for our undertaking . . .

BLIGH'S PRAYER

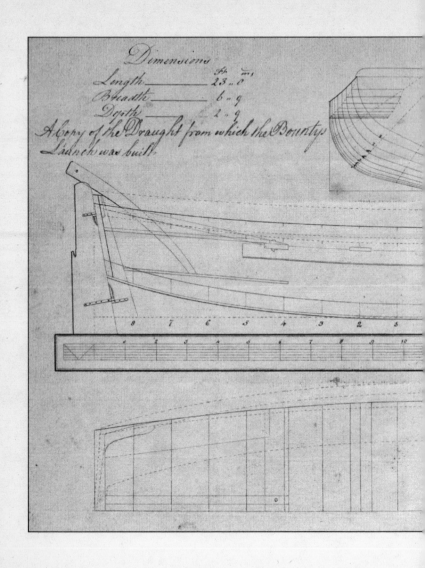

The Bounty's *Launch*

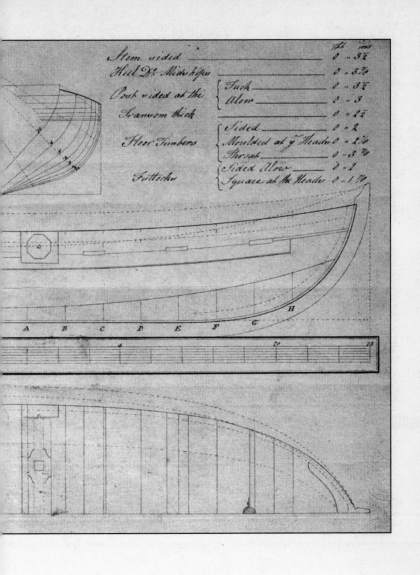

			ft	ins
Stem sided			0	3⅞
Keel Do Midships			0	3¾
Post sided at the	{	Tuck	0	3⅞
		Alow	0	3
Stranson thick			0	2½
Floor Timbers	{	Sided	0	2
		Moulded at ye Heads	0	2½
		Thro' it	0	3¾
Futtocks	{	Sided Alow	0	2
		Square at the Heads	0	1¾

Prologue

Prologue

ALL BUT NAKED, William Bligh stood on the decks of the *Bounty* just before dawn on 28th April, 1789. At the prod of a cutlass to his buttock he climbed over a bulwark and down the ladder into the launch waiting below.

He would never understand how the mutiny happened, and he would never placate his outrage, but it blew up and was over before he'd had time to gather his wits. It was as though God made him step aside while some squalid matter outside his responsibility was attended to, and when he was allowed back it just happened that his ship and most of its crew had vanished.

Of course, for the rest of his life he would be Bligh of the *Bounty*, and people who had forgotten his great feats of survival and heroism would, on meeting him, seize upon some small, lurid detail from the ship's legend and pester him with it. More than that, he would achieve a status restricted to a diverse and not always salubrious gang of characters in history—he would become a living metaphor. Cruelty, violence, rigour and discipline: these would be the qualities one used the word 'Bligh' to encompass. He would live with it—there would be greater and sadder burdens to bear—yet never weary of trying to give some justice back to his name. In the future, people would not understand his fussiness, his pedantry and passion for detail, or his intense personal sense that the *enemy*—

whatever or whoever it might be—was still there, even though it was less powerful, and even less definable than before. Bligh would not want adulation, just respect, and he would never be able to figure out how that came so easily to so many undeserving men, yet was denied to him.

Through long afternoons of tortuous self-examination in the days to come, he would cast his mind back, searching for the key to his personal failure and always—against his will it seemed—he returned to Kealakekua Bay in Hawaii ten years earlier, to the day when Cook was killed.

CHAPTER 1

Kealakekua Bay

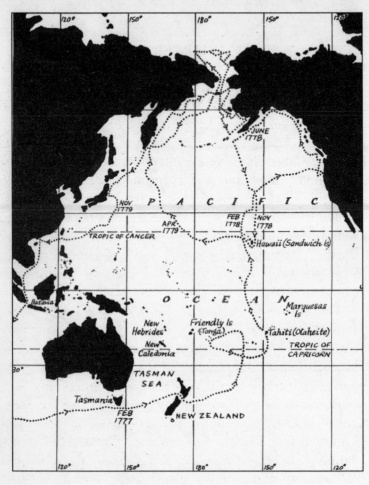

Cook's third voyage in the Pacific

IN 1776, WHEN twenty-two-year-old William Bligh joined James Cook's third voyage to the Pacific as Master on the *Resolution*, the world was still young. Most of it remained secret except to the imagination. Parts of the coast of New Holland (Australia) had been but roughly sketched and its interior, like Africa's and America's, was a mystery. Asia, if better known, was still full of possibilities, and scant, albeit tantalising, details were just beginning to come through about the Pacific. A British sailor could watch Plymouth slowly fade from view and feel that from here on his life was out of God's hands.

Therein lay the source of so much of Cook's great reputation. He held a beacon up to the void and when he asked men to follow him in they understood that if he didn't know the way he knew what it promised. He had gone further than anyone else, seen things only the most blasphemous would contemplate, and he had always returned. In the 1770s the dockside taverns still hummed with stories of expeditions that had failed, or simply vanished. If scurvy didn't get them the ice-floes of the north would freeze them in or the tropical heat would send them mad. George Anson had sailed into the Pacific with six ships and returned with just one, and over a thousand of his crew had died, and that, they all said, was bound to happen. James Cook was a hero not just for his discoveries but for his wisdom, compassion and the fact that his crew returned better men than when they'd left. To be appointed Master of the *Resolution*, the ship Cook would himself captain, was an intimidating honour and it was a role William Bligh would fiercely treasure.

The Master in the Georgian Navy was the Warrant Officer responsible for navigating the ship. He had to know how to use the compasses, sextants and quadrants and he had to care for them. He needed to be able to read the heavens and the sea and to work out logarithms and draw charts, and all this knowledge was useless if he didn't know how a ship was rigged, how the anchors worked, who to call on in particular emergencies, and the difference between the Etesian and the Trade winds. He had to be a mathematician and craftsman, scientist and labourer, and if he did his job badly he imperilled everyone else's life. That was the average Master in the Georgian Navy. Cook's Master was expected to be a lot more.

What first drew Bligh to Cook's attention was his skill as a cartographer. In that regard Bligh was thoroughly precocious and, like Cook, self-taught. At twenty-two he'd been exposed to too much to be a youth any longer—the Navy had that effect on people—although a certain callowness remained. He was a man Cook could nurture. They were artists really, but the end they struggled for was indisputable fact. Not beauty but truth, sensitivity not in feeling but in judgment.

The world they were entering had never been mapped before and they were mindful that their perceptions would influence those who came afterwards. From the southern coast of Tasmania to the ice-

choked bays of Alaska, from Christmas Island to
Kuskokwim Bay, Cook sent his Master out to take
soundings and chart the landforms they encountered,
and the route the expedition took would henceforth be
marked with the Captain's tributes—Bligh's Cap,
Bligh Island, Bligh Entrance, Bligh Sound.

With a delicate, spidery hand Bligh would first draw
the lie of the land as it looked from his dinghy rocking
among the waves, careful to darken the sides of
mountains where the shadows cast from clouds fell and
to give darker greens to those parts where the bush or
the jungle appeared thickest. He had to work fast
because out in the open a few drops splashing across
the bow or falling from the sky could destroy a day's
work. In the South Seas a distant black cloud could
swell up to a typhoon in a matter of minutes. Having
taken soundings and measured the angles of promontories and any other unusual features, he waited
until night, back on board, when he would light the oil-
lamps and transfer the coastal view to a bird's-eye
projection—useful for a sailor trying to make his way
through a treacherous obstacle course. He drew maps,
sketching the shape of every significant feature from a
rock jutting out of the water to the smallest sand-bar,
yet he could only provide glimpses. Where he couldn't
proceed any further the pencil stopped and the land
fell away to oblivion. He had to leave Adventure Bay
and many islands on the way incomplete and unful-
filled, aware there was so much more to do.

Bligh and Edgar, Master of the second ship, the
Discovery, were also expected to keep records of the
ships' stores. Every so often they'd be sent down to

check on the supplies of bread and other foods, mark down and throw out the rotten stuff. That way their knowledge of an expedition's logistics was developed. Cook, after all, was the revolutionary who introduced sauerkraut and lime juice to fight scurvy, insisted on his crew washing themselves and their possessions, and started the practice of dancing on the open decks for exercise. An expedition's success depended upon a lot more than reaching a certain point and turning back. It needed healthy bodies and clear minds. William Bligh learnt that and a lot more as Master of the *Resolution*. When the time would come for him to lead his own, humble little expedition to Otaheite (Tahiti) he would bring to bear on it everything the Great Man had taught him.

The world they entered on the voyage had all the strangeness of a dream. Leaving Capetown, the ships headed south, through the Crozet Archipelago, to sail in a roughly straight line towards Van Diemen's Land (Tasmania), still believed to be joined to the mainland. Entering the Pacific by its southern doorway they were to head north, to the very top, to make one last search for the legendary north-west passage to Europe, the possible existence of which had obsessed explorers, philosophers and merchants since Columbus returned from the West Indies nearly three hundred years earlier. As with Cook's second expedition, which had searched for the great southern continent, the promise of something fabled and elusive inspired the crew as they entered uncharted waters.

Chilled by winds blowing untrammelled from the

Antarctic they reached the Kerguelen Islands, halfway between Africa and Australia and discovered by a Frenchman just four years earlier. If there was anywhere on earth more desolate and forbidding, no one had yet heard about it. Wrapped in constant fog, they were islands not so much of grass as lichen, not of trees but stunted, weatherbeaten scrub, where the bare rocks glistened with a permanent varnish of ice and the penguins had such minimal experience of humanity they allowed themselves to be punched unconscious by yodelling seamen.

At Adventure Bay, on the skeletal Bruny Island just off Van Diemen's Land, Bligh busied himself with taking soundings and charting the jagged shoreline while the Captain and the other officers entered the giant forest and met the inhabitants. Apart from Omai—the Otaheitean returning home after a couple of years' exposure to English high society—the only other Indians he'd encountered had been the forlorn and dishevelled creatures on display in fairground tents and the strange types who attached themselves to whaling crews and roamed around foreign ports. Here he saw the smoke from Indians' fires wafting among the giant trees and dense bush, and once or twice he saw a group of them in the distance, utterly naked and unadorned as they conferred on the beach with the Captain. Bligh knew that if he went to join the Captain, Cook would make formal introductions and smooth over any culturally delicate matters, but it mattered more to him that he complete the mapping. His efforts so far had met with approval and he was being given more responsibilities and greater areas to chart. This would be his contribution to the expedition. It would be how he would make his mark.

In Otaheite they saw the aftermath of a human sacrifice. Taken by canoe to a nearby island, Cook and several of his crew were led up the beach to a morai (a sacred burial place) where four priests and a trussed-up corpse waited before a crowd of several hundred men (but no women). Amid long prayers, the stench of rancid pig meat and small, obscure offerings, the body was covered with leaves, then uncovered and laid out along the water's edge while one of its eyes was removed, wrapped in a green leaf and presented to an officiating priest. As a kingfisher in a nearby tree announced with its song the presence of a god, the body was carried to the morai, another priest chanted a prayer and drums slowly beat. The body was placed in a shallow pit on the morai, a dog was slaughtered, its entrails thrown on a fire, and the god was invited to eat. This being his third visit to Otaheite, Cook knew better than to be offended.

From Otaheite the ships moved north to Hawaii and when the *Resolution* and the *Discovery* dropped their anchors in the bay in January 1779, tens of thousands of Hawaiians in feathers and flowers cheered them in. It was a successful visit. But when they returned with a broken mast in February, the bay was deserted. Only one or two canoeists went about their business close by the shore; the sullen atmosphere was incomprehensible to the white men. The same chiefs who only weeks before had treated Cook as though he were some deity, had dressed him in a long feather cloak, presented great banquets of pig and taro and prostrated themselves to the chant of 'Orono, Orono, Orono', were now either away or reluctant to show themselves. When they did finally meet Cook the day after his arrival, he and his men weren't able to interpret their sudden change in character, but it was something like embarrassment, with a threatening edge.

The Europeans hadn't intended to return, but a few days out from the islands a storm had shattered the foremast of the *Resolution* and, knowing nothing of what lay ahead, they had no choice but to come back to land to repair it.

The commoners carried on as though all was normal. Two enormous women, boar tusk bracelets clanking, braided hair and bone necklaces flopping against their heavy breasts, sauntered about the decks, aloof to the crewmen's protests as they ran their fingers across metal and through cloth, and held glass objects up to the light. They left, returning later that day with their even larger sister, and all departed laden with magnifying lenses and coloured beads.

All the usual annoyances were present: the sailor who cheerfully ignored the boundaries of decorum and the quick-fingered Hawaiian whose every move needed close attention. And then there was Pareea. Small, ingratiating and sinister, he was an Arioi (somewhere between a priest and a political heavy) who enjoyed making trouble. The first time the ships had anchored in the bay and the Hawaiians paddled out to trade, he had interfered in the bargaining to warn one of his people to get an advance price on his pig before he sold it. The sailor involved in the dealing had pushed Pareea away and within hours a tabu had been placed over the bay preventing all Hawaiians from entering it.

On one occasion he found pleasure in putting an Hawaiian up to steal some tools, then making a show of chasing the thief and retrieving the items. In the late afternoon, on his suggestion, a boy who'd kept an eye on the blacksmith's work area ran forward, snatched a pair of tongs and dived into the water, swimming quickly to a nearby canoe as the crewmen went through the slow process of lowering a cutter boat to give chase. By the time they reached the beach the thief had vanished into the hilly jungle. A crowd armed with stones was on hand to meet the Europeans.

Earlier in the morning, a group of sailors had rowed across to another part of the bay and hired some Hawaiians to help replenish their water barrels from a spring bubbling up from a fissure. While they worked, a group of chiefs approached from across the beach and ordered their people away from the white men, a confrontation that had obliged Cook, Lieutenant James King and a number of marines to come across from the ships and post a guard. Cook was reluctantly adamant. In this unpleasant atmosphere, if there was any trouble the marines were to shoot. Dutifully King directed that they load their muskets with ball, not shot—in other words, they would shoot to kill.

This was how Cook came to be on the beach when the tongs were stolen, how he managed to be close by when the pursuers landed their craft, and how he ended up leading the chase for the supposed thief for three miles along narrow tracks winding through tangled bush and up slimy hillsides, while Hawaiians amused themselves feeding him false directions.

Back on the beach, Pareea arrived just as the *Discovery*'s Master, Edgar, took possession of the canoe the thief had paddled across from the boat. It was a variation on Cook's approach—to assume an inherent spirit of enterprise in the Hawaiians, and see both thieving and hostage-taking as business, nothing personal. Everything could be traded. Sometimes, for a diplomat like Cook experienced in their ways, it worked. Unfortunately the canoe Edgar intended holding was Pareea's, not the thief's, and Edgar was not diplomatic. When Pareea grabbed him he cracked an oar across the Hawaiian's head, and suddenly the crewmen were under attack, beaten back into the water by stone-throwing Hawaiians who then ransacked the abandoned cutter until Pareea, recovered, stopped them. He didn't want a fight—not yet and not one he was responsible for—but for now his strategy had worked. The Hawaiians became more impudent and the sailors bad-tempered, and the tension simmered.

The broken mast had been sent to shore along with the astronomers' tents and equipment. This was a scientific voyage, and every opportunity to examine, catalogue and analyse was taken. As with Cook's previous voyages, some men would plot the position of the stars, others would document what scraps of language they found, and there was the endless garden of new plants to cut up, sketch and name. The place they chose to pitch the tents this time was a morai.

If Polynesia was the fabulous kingdom of the noble savage for the fashionable European philosophers of the age, the morais appealed to the tastes of the equally fashionable Gothic horror novelists. For the artists on board with the Pacific explorers they were full of menace. Raised platforms of stone, they were burial grounds, houses of the dead, not quite temples, not quite tombs, surrounded by brightly painted and carved poles and piled with skulls, bones and other relics. They were sacred places, protected by tabu, where the spirit might safely leave the body, and where human sacrifices, if necessary, were performed. In this alien world where free love was as natural as cannibalism, the morai was an altar to gods whose closest European cousins were the pagan deities driven out in the Old Testament.

The artists were artists after all and found skulls romantic, if not utterly poetic, but to other men of the Georgian Navy who'd already seen more of the earth than anyone else alive, it was just more native peculiarity. The great advantage of the morai for storing equipment was that the locals needed courage to enter it. The polished boxes full of shiny brass instruments were safer in the morai than on board the ships.

So on the third night King and his marines had camped in the morai, with a few minor disturbances, and just after dawn he rowed across to the *Resolution*. Cook was loading his double-barrelled musket as he climbed up on to the deck, and other sailors were arming themselves, packing powder and loading the cannons. The lieutenant needed to shout to have his questions answered, but eventually the Captain responded. At some point during the night someone had slipped out, cut free one of the *Discovery*'s cutter boats and stolen it. Not a gewgaw or a gimcrack but a whole damned boat.

Cook was baffled by the new violence in the Hawaiians' behaviour. He appreciated that he, his scientists and all the amateur ethnographers on board had scarcely touched the surface of Polynesian culture. It remained impenetrable and misunderstood, even to someone as patient and engaged as he was. But by now he was a tired man. He had spent ten years out in these waters and his tolerance was exhausted. On this day he no longer cared for the details of Hawaiian culture when it seemed like so much pig-headed caprice. Words, tact, negotiations: all merely delayed an inevitable confrontation, and if he had transgressed some tabu or tribal custom it didn't matter anymore to try to understand what it was.

If the Hawaiians wanted a fight he would no longer meet them on their terms, but bring all the force of his firepower into play. With that in mind and his voice weary with impatience, he ordered four boats—two from each ship—to fan out across the mouth of the bay and set up a cordon. No canoes were to leave. Any that tried were to be shot at and sunk. In charge of the launch in the south-east corner of the cordon sat William Bligh, now twenty-five years old.

Somebody fired before he did. Bligh was as sure of that as he could be of anything that day. Someone from the other boat panicked when he saw the Hawaiians on the beach move towards their canoes and fired. One of the Hawaiians grabbed at his buttock where he'd been shot and at that very second he was the one Bligh had in his sights. He pulled the trigger as the Hawaiian was sinking and the shot knocked him flat and lifeless. As though it had been orchestrated, every other gun on the boats erupted and as the smoke and thunder blew back across the bay he could make out several figures sprawled across the sand, a crimson stain spreading towards the water. He was—he was later led to understand—the highest ranking person in the two boats, therefore in command, but he didn't give any orders until they'd packed their powder and fired again, and by that time they were only having target practice at a handful of corpses, the unharmed and the wounded having disappeared into the bush.

If it had been up to Bligh he would not have fired, and yet he didn't regret it. Say what people would about natives, about 'Indians', a danger nipped in the bud was no danger at all. To be sure, Bligh himself would not have moved until he was certain the Hawaiians were running for their canoes but he had not tried to convince anyone they weren't. The thieving, the rudeness, the stone throwing—the Hawaiians had started it and there were thousands of them to deal with. A couple of good musket volleys could be far more eloquent than any hostage-taking or parleying with the king.

When the gunfire started up at another part of the bay, he didn't think it had any connection with his own area. Not then. He turned to see what was happening in the distance, but it was too far to identify anyone clearly. Hordes of Indians were screaming and hurling rocks at a handful of sailors struggling through the water towards the pinnace, and several white men were being torn apart on the beach. Then the gunfire itself seemed to quicken with fear, and the Hawaiian cries acquired a new, desperate pitch. It was no ordinary skirmish, but it wasn't until he was on board the ship a couple of hours later that the rumours that had been passed along the cordon were confirmed.

They'd stabbed the Captain in the back. That was the worst part—well, that and the fact that they had hacked up his body and taken it away. Cook had tried pleading for peace, but then he'd turned his back on people who had no sense of courage or honour. By this stage in the expedition the Europeans had seen enough of the Pacific to leave little to their imaginations as to what happened when the Hawaiians ran off with a corpse—but the back-stabbing! Here were people who only weeks ago had treated the Captain like a god, and now they cut him down the coward's way. There were some on the ship arguing that the Captain had made a mistake when he shot at one of the Indians and missed, and others who said he should never have turned his back on them. What did it matter? It was a man's right to make a mistake and now he'd made it, now he'd paid the ultimate price, what consolation was it to debate what that mistake might have been?

There was work to be done. The *Resolution*'s mast and the astronomers' equipment were still up at the morai, and a crowd of Hawaiians had gathered at a safe distance from Lieutenant King and the six marines guarding the site, threatening them with gestures and shouts. Thinking they were about to be attacked,

Captain Clerke of the *Discovery*, taking command, ordered a couple of cannon fired towards them. One ball split a coconut palm and the other shattered a boulder, but neither scared anyone off.

Actually, up at the morai Cook's death had produced a strange state between tension and calm. Watching the rowboats silently cross between the ships, King knew without being told that the Captain had been killed. The Hawaiians also knew that something was wrong, but until they had the full story, both sides maintained a desultory communication—threatening one another at the faintest suspicion of trouble, then resuming friendly conversation. Under these conditions King sent a marine across to tell Clerke to desist with the cannon and Clerke responded by sending Bligh back to tell King to strike camp and prepare to ferry the mast back.

King left Bligh in charge and returned to the ships. Educated, intellectual and as fascinated by Polynesian culture as he was by British political debate and scientific discovery, James King suffered from a problem common among well-bred youth. He put too much faith in Rousseau's ideas of the goodness of human nature. He imagined others on the expedition shared his educated passions, that they felt the same profound sense of history, that someone like William Bligh would understand the proper way to behave in these circumstances. He had barely reached the ships before the first musket shots echoed across from the morai.

On the cutter, watching the battle on the beach, Bligh had heard the clapping together of stones as the

Hawaiians triumphed over the body, and it had chilled him. It was as though a thousand skeletons had risen to applaud, and before the sound had died away he was full of revulsion. Now he was up on the morai, surrounded by yellow bones and skulls and the hideous grins of the painted posts. A safe distance away and obscured by the jungle, Hawaiians excited by the killing had gathered and every so often their voices rose in a unified and unintelligible chatter. He was no more or less religious than he ever had to be, but even a mind as open to skepticism as his had its limits, and here, in the physical presence of death, the chatter sounded thoroughly pagan, blasphemous and frightening.

Taking their cue from him the marines took up positions behind rocks and trees. When the first stone whistled derisively up into the morai they caught a flash of retreating brown skin and fired. The Hawaiians well knew by now just how long it took to reload a musket with buck and ball, and before the gunsmoke lifted Bligh and his men had to cower as a barrage of stones rattled into the burial ground. Then, with the warriors in the open, they fired again.

Along the wall of the morai facing the sea a group of warriors crept, thinking they could take it by stealth, but they were caught out and gunned down as they ran.

It bothered Bligh, this shooting at unarmed men, but he suffered no illusions. Indeed, there had been times when the Captain and some of his officers had shown a compassion that reflected a poor sense of judgment in regards to Indians. Times when a good volley of muskets would have said so much more than empty or misunderstood gestures. He wasn't for killing them the way the Spanish butchered people in America, but a gun was useful for imposing respect, and it was just possible that had the Captain used one more liberally he would be back on board the *Resolution* and he, Bligh, wouldn't be here now.

An Indian, his left knee shattered by a musket shot, limped from tree to tree towards a friend collapsed upon a bush and bleeding heavily from a wound in the belly. As he bent to take his hand Bligh spied them, aimed and fired, catching the limping man on the hip and spinning him around to crash into the bushes. He reloaded as a stone thudded into the tree trunk a mere inch above his head, and when he next turned back the Indian was on his feet and reaching for his friend once more. Raising the musket to aim again, Bligh was about to pull the trigger when King reappeared, ordering the men to cease firing. The Hawaiian lifted his injured friend to his feet, took a couple of steps and fell dead. Beating a retreat down the twisted, vine-choked trails, the Englishmen heard the gunfire splutter up as marines landed on the beach and attacked a force of warriors running across the sand. Before King could successfully call a truce several more Hawaiians fell mortally wounded. Patches greasy with blood and flesh stained the white beach.

The following evening two Hawaiians rowed out to the *Resolution* with a bundle of cloth containing the deboned thigh of Captain Cook. The next morning a man wearing the Captain's hat threw stones from his canoe and slapped his buttocks in contempt. The day after that several crewmen went ashore, burned down a village, caught two Hawaiians and decapitated them. They returned with the heads and strung them up for everyone to see. On the Friday, two days later, a chief came to the *Resolution* with more parcels containing Cook's scalp, the bones of his thighs, arms and legs, and his hands. The rest of the body had been divided up. One chief received his head, another his hair, a third his lower jawbone. Nothing else remained.

CHAPTER 2

The *Bounty*

FROM THE SANDWICH Isles, the ships moved eastwards to the North American coast, to Nootka Sound and the Alaskan summer, where Bligh proved himself as a navigator and cartographer. The expedition progressed through the Bering Straits, into the harrowing fog and crystal atmosphere of the Arctic, then down past Siberian Kamchatka and its dim, tenuous reminders of Europe. In Japan, Macao, Vietnam, Krakatoa, Batavia, the world revealed itself so artfully a man could scarcely distinguish between the exotic and the everyday. 'England', the one constant fact in Bligh's life, was becoming vague and confused. Did that smell drifting across a strange Asian port really evoke grimy old Plymouth with the sprats drying on the sea wall, or the tart odours he'd experienced in some primitive's hut a few months back as the wind outside pierced the hides covering the doorway?

After the *Resolution* returned to Britain, Cook's incomplete journal of the voyage was published. As with his journals for the first and second voyages (and any book that promised first-hand accounts of Otaheite and its women), the heavy, leather-bound edition lavishly illustrated with engravings was a publisher's dream. Death had only enhanced the explorer's fame and if people didn't actually read the book they knew what it contained. Bligh, of course, obtained a copy.

On the title-page, permanently there for all to see,

was the statement: *Illustrated with Maps and Charts, from the original drawings made by Lieut. Henry Roberts, under the direction of Captain COOK.*

His hand shaking with a rage he could barely contain, Bligh drew a thick, angry line through the sentence and wrote in the margin: *None of the Maps and Charts in this publication are from the original drawings of Lieut. Henry Roberts, he did no more than copy the original ones from Captain Cook who besides myself was the only person that surveyed & laid the Coast down, in the* Resolution. *Every Plan & Chart from C. Cook's death are exact copies of my works.*

Wm Bligh

It was an odd and desperate appeal, made in private and without any hope justice would be done. Everybody else, it seemed, had profited from the voyage except himself. If there was one thing more saleable than a slightly salacious description of Otaheitean women it was an eye-witness's version of what had happened at Kealakekua Bay. It was an insult to the Great Man's memory that some people, such as the surgeon's assistants William Ellis and David Samwell, who in his opinion had made but small contributions to the expedition, should now rake in the cash based on their accounts of something they'd barely glimpsed in the distance. As he went through the book, annotating the pages with the absolute truth according to William Bligh, the pen hissed with a seething anger . . .

The opposite is from C. Cook's original survey, which agrees nearly with mine except in laying down Anderson's Isle—Here is a gross mistake for Anderson's & the East end of Clerk's Island is one and the same land, and how they have blundred to lay them down as two I cannot conceive.

Wm Bligh

Everybody else had profited. They made money and were promoted. Everybody but himself, and here he was even denied credit for his maps and charts—the very work the Great Man had praised him for. Of course Cook would never have written that Henry Roberts made the drawings—Cook was a great man because he was wise and just—but he, of course, hadn't been around to complete his journal and arrange for its publication. Clerke had died from complications courtesy of tuberculosis in Siberia a couple of months after Cook. This left the responsibility to Lieutenant King. More bile could not be reserved for another individual than Bligh kept for that pompous and effeminate sneak—a man who knew a little about sailing but a lot more about sycophancy and the prestige of a respectable family. A pretentious egg-head who could talk for hours about theory but couldn't put it to practical use.

C. King might well say it was fatigues he underwent for he never bore any or was he capable—His whole account if he had been a seaman he would have been ashamed to have related, but as he conceived few would read it who had been present with him, he had . . .

It was a plot against himself, Bligh had no doubt, and he could even locate the moment its seed had been sown. He had heard a rumour along the wharves and in the taverns that in the minutes before the cannibals ran their spears into Cook's back there'd been the probability the dispute would be resolved—the Great

Man had raised his hands and the Islanders had stopped to listen, but then someone in the cordon of boats had fired their musket and killed a chief. An eye for an eye being the savages' code, they'd only done what came naturally. This was the rumour and now Bligh's imagination spun a lurid fantasy based on his dislike of James King. If King had disliked him before, just in a general way, Kealakekua Bay had given him a focus for active hatred. It didn't matter that Bligh hadn't fired the first musket. King wanted someone to blame and there he was, William Bligh, sitting in the cutter with a smoking gun in his hand.

Poor Bligh. King didn't hate him. He didn't like him but he didn't hate him. King had been up at the morai, too busy keeping the peace to know or care who fired the first shot, and he was too perceptive to imagine it made any difference. If there was a reason why he didn't like Bligh it had more to do with that time he'd returned to the morai, well after Cook's death, to see his good work undone by a few gun-happy thugs and Master Bligh blasting away at a poor wounded Indian who was only showing everyone what good Christian actions were all about.

In the seven years following the return of the *Resolution* in 1780, Bligh had a number of positions, but none of much importance. He felt belittled and humiliated that his talents went unrecognized in the long years that passed before he was given command of the *Bounty*. He didn't have the proper social gifts in the right amounts.

After Cook's death King, Ellis, Samwell and Gore all

appeared to be walking along a career path that was gilt-edged and easy on the legs while he had to struggle, and it had nothing to do with talent or hard work. Not being especially religious, he couldn't blame God, yet he did feel that the obstruction was intangible and outside his control.

So it was that when in 1787 Sir Joseph Banks at last proposed that Bligh captain a small ship out to Otaheite, to collect breadfruit which could be grown and fed to the plantation slaves in the West Indies, the delighted Bligh didn't imagine it was a run-of-the-mill voyage that would have little consequence if it failed. He was at last being given the opportunity to prove himself, to show the world that everything he learned from Cook had been learned for a reason. He was, after all, one of the very few men who had the skill and experience to lead an expedition into the Pacific, and to bring it out again.

Everything he had learned from his time on the *Resolution* was dredged up, including Cook's insistent pronouncements on the health of the crew, and so he decided he would institute three watches a day instead of two—giving the men shorter work hours and longer sleeps. He hired half-blind Michael Byrne not for his sailing but for his fiddling skills, so that every night there'd be a few galliards and tarantellas to get the joints creaking. Bligh would feed his men pumpkin, spruce beer, even scurvy grass—anything to chase off the dreaded blight—and he'd spare them the injury of flogging, a cruel and useless waste of energy. Any smart captain could see the damage flogging did to his men.

It broke their spirit and created hatreds, and out on the high seas cruelty could have a bitter reward. If he successfully completed the breadfruit task and returned with all his crew alive, the personal glory would be considerable.

Those long, lean and sometimes frightening years after he returned from the Pacific could never be justified, but the pain could ease, the memory could fade.

Cynics—especially those among the expedition's commercially-minded sponsors—might have found Bligh's excitement poignant, considering the cheap ambitions behind the expedition, but the crew signed on in an atmosphere of good-natured optimism and a raring to unfurl the sails. The word 'Otaheite' had that effect on sailors, and these were no mere Jack-Tars to William Bligh but good men, fine seamen, as sharp a crew as any he could ask for among the Admiralty's long list of whoresons, badmash, drunkards and skunks. He wrote so and he said it to their faces before departure. Such open-hearted affection, however, only invites men to test it.

When the *Bounty* left Spithead on 23rd December 1787, the brisk winter winds turned ugly and within three days ominous storms had broken spars and smashed chains, washing supplies overboard. A few weeks out to sea and whatever warmth existed between Bligh and John Fryer, the *Bounty*'s Master and his second-in-command, had deteriorated. They were heading for their first confrontation, the first of many.

John Fryer's portrait by Gaetano Calleyo shows a man in middle age, his grey hair receding, his

John Fryer c. 1807 by Gaetano Calleyo

complexion ruddy, his eyes watery with world-weariness. He is otherwise unremarkable, his face like so many hanging from the walls of Georgian mansions, the stolid and bucolic farming man, the grain merchant or horse dealer, unimpressed by flights of the imagination, obsessed with the smallest details of daily business.

John Fryer came from Wells-next-the-Sea, a Norfolk port not far from the Wash, where samphire grew thick among the marshes, the eelmen trolled through the sloblands in their rickety little craft, and nearby Holland made its influence felt in the high-pitched roofs and gables of the houses. In the countryside behind the town, wheat, barley and oats were harvested and stored in the portside granaries, and oysters were gathered from the rocks around the shore. Along the waterfront, where the gulls nose-dived for pilchards and the boats creaked against their moorings, small, curious seafaring industries thrived, enjoying the years before the Industrial Revolution closed them down. Tholes, boomkins, catheads and spirkets were made and sold by specialized artisans, and when work was quiet smacksmen loitered on the road outside the warehouses of chandlers and coopers. The people of Norfolk spoke differently to other Britons, and the Norfolkers around the ports spoke another language again, the secret codes of ancient trades.

John Fryer's father was a blockmaker: a craftsman who hand-carved the pulley systems for hoisting sails. If John dreamed of going to sea in a frigate he would have had to travel down to Great Yarmouth actually to see one. In Wells it was herring boats and luggers, the stuff of modest ambition.

He began in the Navy where all boys from his background did—at rock bottom. His life was to proceed in the normal way for a man of such position in the eighteenth century—a series of accidents and tragedies that may have tempered the mettle of a visionary but tended to drive the more ordinary towards bitterness and self-pity.

In 1776, when he was twenty-four, his ship ran foul of a French privateer in the Mediterranean and he spent fifteen months in a Marseilles gaol, biding his time until there was a formal exchange of prisoners between England and France. There was a small reward for suffering in the damp and dark, though. On the way home he so impressed the ship's officers with his seamanship that they listed him in the books as a Master's Mate—his first ever promotion.

In 1780 he passed his examinations to be a Master and was given a warrant for the *Camel*, which promptly sank; hardly auspicious for a man intending to make a career out of navigation. It would be another six years before he was again given the same honour and responsibility—this time on the *Bounty*. In the interim he married Ann Sporne, who died in 1784 without children, and three years later he remarried, to Mary Tinkler. She was pregnant when the *Bounty* left Spithead and a few months later gave birth to a boy who would not see his father until he was three.

Fryer enlisted unaware that his Captain's enthusiasm masked resentment and fears of failure. His own were so entrenched he'd come to think the Good Lord had singled him out uniquely for persecution. It had been six years now since he'd mastered a ship the size of the *Bounty*, and though he'd obviously redeemed himself in the eyes of the Admiralty he'd not in his own. Death, prison, the naturally violent ways of the Navy, slow and bitter progress: they'd all scarred him. They'd worn him down and robbed him of the energy for pleasure. He disliked Bligh's confidence and he refused to see why the Plymouthman should have been Captain by now. He, Fryer, was two years older and, but for bad luck and timing, would have been just as good for the job. He knew as much about navigation as Bligh and he'd paid a heavier price for his knowledge.

In the Georgian Navy the path upwards was tough, ruthless and slow. Those who came in at the bottom, who had to graduate first to being Able Seamen, had to demonstrate they could fulfil certain tasks, and might spend years doing so. They suffered the Captain's temper, the floggings and the beatings. They worked the longest hours at the most gruelling chores, ate the maggots and the weevils, slept in tiny cots and hammocks in the dampest and coldest part of the hold. Above them in rank and permitted certain creature comforts were the Midshipmen, the 'young gentle-men'. They might be the sons of naval men, or of the generally wealthy, an errant lad in danger of squan-dering the family fortune or a bright spark destined to be a leader. Spared from physical labour and allowed in some circumstances to embark with a kit full of personal luxuries, they learned that ritual humiliation was good training for an officer and enjoyed the cruel games they were allowed to play upon the sailors ranked below them. The system worked on the simple rule of thumb that class hatred was an efficient form of social control.

For someone with aptitude but no social connections, like John Fryer, the climb through the ranks was formidable. After years spent having his palms rubbed raw by hawser ropes and his back bent by heavy loads and cramped space, being beaten by drunken Captains and shamed by precious Midshipmen, he could apply for his Master's Certificate and sit the exam. If he passed he came in at sixth rate (at about three shillings a day) and worked his way gradually up to first rate (five shillings). He might be rewarded then with a post-captaincy, but by this stage he would be old and injured by his work and there were few openings other than short-hauls around the coast or the odd voyage across to America.

In this climate promotion was a desperate matter and certain positions on board ship carried an implication—not a written certainty—that the man awarded it would have his rank improved when he returned home. Such a position was the charge of a watch—responsibility for the ship while it sailed or lay anchored at night. It was a sign the Captain was impressed enough to share his duties with the sailor and would declare so when he handed his log to the Admiralty. Outside of Tenerife William Bligh bypassed John Fryer for the job and gave it to the Master's Mate instead—to Fletcher Christian.

That stung. It had to be taken as a personal insult, even if it was the Midshipmen who were traditionally offered the position. Fair enough if this was a short haul up to the Baltic or even a lengthy voyage under correct naval conditions, but it was neither.

Much about the *Bounty* expedition was unusual, perhaps because it was done on the cheap. There were no marines to enforce the Captain's authority, as was normally the case in the Navy, and there was no hierarchy of officers between the Captain and his Master. There were no secondary missions to discover new lands, to keep an eye out for missing explorers or to observe French machinations in the region. Nothing that might divert attention from the purely commercial interest.

Fryer now was to demonstrate that for all his short-comings, his low self-esteem and his bitterness, he was not poor on cunning. As Bligh had indirectly under-mined his authority, so he would undermine the Captain's, and here was a Captain jealously protective of his reputation, who couldn't hide the value he put on smooth sailing in all matters.

Able Seaman Matthew Quintal had given Fryer a bit of lip. Somewhere along the way the sailor who would later be hacked up with an axe while he lay drunk and hallucinating on Pitcairn Island crossed the Master, and though their exchange was never recorded it gave Fryer the opportunity to report him to Bligh for 'mutinous behaviour'. Even though the Captain down-graded the charge to 'insolence', Fryer had responded very much within the letter of the law and, as the incident was to be officially recorded in the log, gave the Captain no choice but to punish the man. On 10th of March Quintal was stripped down and strung up to a lattice frame and the boatswain flogged him twenty-four times. The cat—a broad, thick strap of leather cut into strips—sliced through Quintal's back splashing his blood across the deck and into the Captain's grim face.

Fryer had forced Bligh to take up the cat and spoil his clean record on floggings, spread a little animosity about, and given Quintal and his cronies good cause to despise the Captain—and he, Fryer, thought he had escaped unblemished.

Not quite.

A little over a year later Matthew Quintal stood by Fletcher Christian's side and pushed men on to the launch to join Bligh. They both knew exactly how Fryer felt about Bligh. If they'd wanted a good navigator to take them back to Otaheite and wherever else their hearts led them, it wouldn't have been hard to persuade him to come along. But neither of them wanted to share Otaheite with John Fryer any more. Christian neither liked nor trusted him and Quintal's back was an ugly knot of scar tissue. A slow death on the high seas, cramped in a tiny boat with the man he openly hated, seemed adequate revenge for the flogging he'd engineered.

Fryer put up a feeble protest, suggesting it wouldn't be long before everyone was friends again. Quite rightly he was ignored. From the time he'd been woken up by Quintal and John Sumner and told he was now a prisoner, he'd stepped back from the drama as though waiting for someone else to decide his fate.

He'd even thought up a plan whereby he got the best of both worlds, remaining on board to see to it the mutineers got themselves drunk so he could rescue the ship. Yet like an earlier instant when he could have knocked Christian over and turned the situation around, nothing came of it. Now as he climbed down the rope ladder and took his place among the others on the launch he hesitated, looking up to the mutineers, but the moment to speak had passed and he sat down.

Bligh followed him. There was a shout to put a musket-ball through the bastard, the rope was cut and the first of the breadfruit plants that the crew chucked over the side struck the water.

Eighteen men went with the Captain in the launch. Some of them would have stood by Bligh through thick and thin because they liked and admired him, some because it was their duty. And some hated him more than the mutineers could have imagined.

They began to sail, stunned, towards a thin finger of smoke on the horizon—a volcano steadily fuming on Tofoa, one of the small islands of Tonga. So the longboat voyage began. At the time, William Bligh was thirty-five years old and he'd been in the Navy for twenty-eight years. He had fought the French, the Spanish and the Dutch, navigated luggers around the English coast and sailed merchant vessels to Jamaica. He was the husband of Betsy and the father of Harriet, Mary and Elizabeth. His hair was black and his complexion pale, almost alabaster: a pudgy baby-face upon which relentless exposure to the foulest weather and the excesses of humanity had so far failed to leave a mark. The voyage he was about to undertake would transform an unremarkable mutiny into a legend, it would elevate him to the stature of a hero, and, inexorably, it would destroy him.

CHAPTER 3

The South Sea

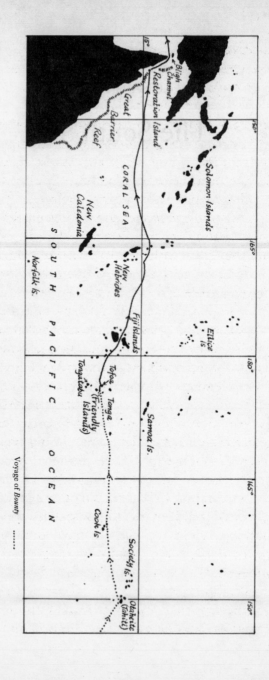

The path of the Bounty from Otaheite to the point of the mutiny, and of the launch to Restoration Island

Voyage of Bounty ·······
Voyage of launch ———

THE DREADFUL SOUND of the clapping of the stones was the rhythm of death. Twelve years earlier, when Bligh aboard the *Resolution* had sailed into nearby Tongatabu, the largest of the Friendly Islands which also included Tonga and Tofoa, he and everyone else had been delighted by King Paulaho's hospitality and appetite. Waddling about the ships with a perpetual grin, the King had devoured a roasted side of pig by himself, then looked hungrily about for more, and if they were worried he would eat his way though the ships' stores they could hardly complain. He had put his islands at their disposal, for the crew to enjoy at their leisure. This had been Cook's second visit to the archipelago, and Bligh had already seen the images from the first—the natives were depicted as Grecian nymphs with little else on their mind but love and beauty, wandering shamelessly through forests unpolluted by European contact. If Bligh was a little too level-headed to be fooled by artists' interpretations, he had to admit there was a certain truth to how they'd described things. The Friendly Isles did have a magical quality about them— something virginal that, if not quite Arcadian, nevertheless struck a chord of nostalgia and yearning: an innocence, a happiness Europe had long ago traded for civilization.

For the first two days after leaving the *Bounty* they had trouble landing the boat. Bligh hadn't seen the western side of Tofoa before and hadn't imagined a shore as barren and rocky as this. Furthermore, storms rained down and the wind raised the waves to pound at the cliffs and narrow, useless ribbons of beach. Tofoa looked more like a North Sea skerry than a South Pacific idyll. Whenever they did land and food-gathering expeditions were sent out, they'd report back with a few miserable coconuts, and scraps of evidence, in the shape of deserted huts and overgrown trails, that the island was inhabited.

Soon after sunrise on the Friday, the men searching for food encountered two men, a woman and a child who came back to the small beach and the cave where the other crewmen huddled. Slowly over the morning other islanders arrived at the beach, bringing coconuts, breadfruit and taro to trade, and a problem made itself apparent in Bligh's mind.

Where was the white men's ship? The question was not asked merely out of curiosity. Repeated enough times it developed a sinister tone and he became aware that a wrong answer—especially an honest one—was an invitation to trouble. *It sunk and we are the only survivors.* What else could he say? Some of the Islanders recognized him, they even asked after Captain Clerke, and they weren't about to think he was here purely by chance. That answer at least would save him from the indignity, if not the danger, of admitting he'd been usurped as Chief, and might open a few doors in some compassionate hearts.

But the Islanders began to grow restless. He could understand only the bare bones of what they were discussing, but he could *feel* what was in their minds. It was there in the sound of their voices and the looks in their eyes, in the brazen, transparent veneer of their friendliness and the unpleasant sensation he felt as, on the Saturday, more and more of them kept appearing on the beach.

What would happen if his men and he were killed? Christian and his dogs would sail back to Otaheite never to be troubled by British law. By the time an official inquiry was established and a ship sent out, the mutineers would have grown old, fat and happy while he, Bligh, would be lucky to be a pile of bleached bones on a morai somewhere—another baffling riddle of the high seas; a vanishing, just like hundreds that had come before him and no longer warranted so much as a footnote in the annals of the Royal Navy. In situations like this, weaker men often made promises to God that if they escaped with their life they would enter the Church, or work for the poor, or they'd make some other hollow sentimental gesture. He made a promise but it was to himself: if he got out of this mess, he would hunt Christian down and bring him to face a British court, British justice and the harshest punishment it reserved for the scum who defied it. Thinking this way of Christian and the filth he'd collected, Bligh felt his resolve harden. These Indians, if they killed him, would not kill a lily-liver.

Bligh wasn't the only one on the launch to have encountered Pacific Islanders before this voyage. William Peckover the gunner and David Nelson the botanist had also sailed with Cook and experienced Polynesian love and bloodshed. Peckover had actually sailed with the Great Man on all three voyages, spoke the language credibly and had been the *Bounty*'s interpreter and trading broker. Neither he nor Nelson were under any illusions as to the Islanders' intentions.

Around noon Bligh served his crewmen their lunch—a piece of breadfruit and some coconut—and several of the chiefs invited him to sit with them to eat. For a while now some of the crowd had sporadically but with increasing enthusiasm been clapping their stones together. All three men knew what it meant, and Nelson leaned forward to whisper to Bligh that the chiefs' invitation was a trap. The moment he was close enough they would grab him. Bligh concurred and remained standing, chewing nervously at his breadfruit.

Over the afternoon, as the sound of the stones grew more boisterous, he sent his men back to the launch, hoping perhaps that if they went slowly enough the Islanders wouldn't notice. But they had, of course, and were now tugging at the line anchoring the boat to the shore with a delinquent insolence. Someone even tried to grab a little notebook of Bligh's from Robert Tinkler's hand as he carried it to the boat, but Peckover intervened with some well-chosen language and the young Midshipman was allowed on his way. By sunset, with that brittle, grating rhythm still echoing off the cliffs, Bligh was left with William Purcell to walk to the launch amidst what he would later describe succinctly as a 'silent kind of horror'.

They were just nineteen men with four cutlasses between them against two or three hundred spirited and contemptuous warriors. It was ten years since Cook's death but Bligh had never forgotten the Great

Man's lessons, including his regard for the people of the Pacific Islands. A good Captain understood their customs might be repulsive and their tempers mercurial, but there was a logic to their culture and only a fool would not try to make sense of it. Cook had the gift, whatever it was—self-possession, sensitivity, compassion—and he could take huge gambles on the Islanders' behaviour and turn them to his advantage. When he had punished his own crewmen for thefts committed by the Islanders he was appealing to an innate quality of justice he sensed in the chieftains, and when he took hostages it was an opening for negotiations.

Now Bligh grabbed a hostage, but the Islander simply shook himself free and ran to stand with the crowd, advancing to the chant of the stones. Bligh remembered all the lessons, but he frustrated himself trying to put them into practice. The gift was not his.

As the hostage wriggled free the stones died away into a stillness built on fear and anticipation.

A chieftain who remembered him from Cook's voyage approached and asked why he didn't spend the night on the island.

'I always sleep on the boat,' Bligh answered in a mix of English, sign language and rudimentary Polynesian.

'Very well,' the chief retorted. 'We will kill you.'

Then the stones began to fall.

The first of them struck him on the shoulder, drawing blood as he reached the water's edge. They were thrown with a practised accuracy intended to cut him down. The others were already on board. Bligh was climbing in when John Norton, the bulky, slow-moving Quartermaster, jumped into the water and ran up to cut the rope mooring the boat to the shore. He had barely done it when he stumbled and the Islanders attacked, beating him to death as the launch drifted loose and the men on board cowered under a barrage of stones that slashed and battered their bodies.

Norton's body was not sacrifice enough for what was a real revelation of the Islanders' feelings for the Europeans. Uninhibited by guns or numbers, they celebrated a rare opportunity to pay back the white men for their diseases, their violence and their ignorance by launching their canoes and pursuing the boat across the water, hurling rocks and terrifying warchants until Bligh started throwing over pieces of clothing that by their precious rarity diverted the warriors, allowing the sailors to pull the launch out to sea and to safety. It was the narrowest of escapes.

Their situation was desperate. At the time of the mutiny they had taken or been given a steering compass, a sextant, a quadrant and a couple of books of nautical tables by which longitude could be worked out (or at least, guessed). They also had Carpenter Purcell's tools, a copper pot, 150 pounds of bread, about thirty pounds of pork, six quarts of rum, six bottles of wine, twenty-eight gallons of water and whatever breadfruit and coconuts they had scrounged from the Tofoans. Other than that they were alone, on an ocean they all knew by now to be vast and empty, like death itself, in a boat that couldn't offer even the flimsiest protection against the storms, the sun and the restless, heaving sea.

There was still Tongatabu and jolly King Paulaho, but as Bligh put this proposal forward John Fryer piped up. When he had come through with Cook, had not Bligh experienced some trouble with the natives?

There had in fact been a few thefts, a spot of bother.

Boatswain William Cole then said he would 'Sooner trust to providence and live on an ounce of bread than go to Tongatabu. They'll cut us all to pieces.'

'Very well,' Bligh answered. 'At two ounces a day there's enough food to last us six weeks, with half a gill of water each. If we put our faith in providence and a fair wind, do we each abide to live on this amount?'

He asked every man the question and made certain they all agreed.

'Then where to? Which way?'

William Peckover, who, if only a Gunner, still had more experience of the Pacific than Bligh, suggested there were just two European settlements within six weeks journey. One was Botany Bay, but the *Bounty* had left England before the new settlement had been founded and they weren't to know whether it still survived. The other was the Dutch colony in Timor.

Using the Hamilton Moore *Practical Navigator and Seaman's New Daily Assistant*, the book of requisite tables, and a pocket watch William Peckover had fortuitously kept to himself, the Captain, Peckover and John Fryer were able to work out how far they were from Timor and whether they had the rations to make it. By that fantastic capacity instilled by years of map-making and navigation, Bligh could imagine a chart unrolling, he could see the way, even some of the landmarks on the 3,500-mile journey, and knew that with effort and luck they might get there. They pointed the boat westward and set the sails.

* * *

AS THEY STEERED the launch towards New Holland the wet season was coming to a late close. Persistent, maddening drizzle was to follow them across the seas and when that abated it was usually taken over by downpours threatening to flood and sink the boat. The morning after they fled Tofoa they were caught in one of the more violent storms—one that forced them to work like fury baling out and very nearly destroyed their supply of bread. The popular image of people in a life-boat trapped and babbling under a merciless sun was far from the truth. Bligh and his men would crave its heat—for three weeks they barely saw the sun. They huddled, shivering in fog as thick as any to be found in London and damp that seemed to seep through to the bones, frightened as starvation and cramp set in on a vessel with no room to stretch out or escape each other's misery.

It was 23 feet long, 6 feet 9 inches across the beam and 2 feet 9 inches deep; a handsome, sturdy, two-masted, lug-rigged, square-sailed ten-seater and something of an extravagance for the *Bounty*. It was a good boat for a grand voyage of exploration: one for a couple of scientists and a party of marines to leave the mother ship in and spend a few days collecting plants upriver, documenting the language of head-hunters or sketching the views of an unknown coast. It was not one for a commercial expedition where the most effort would be spent in the cultivation and transportation of breadfruit, but Bligh had his personal dreams: he'd insisted on a good launch to explore, map and discover, and the sponsors had indulged him. It was fortuitous. Had Christian been heartless enough to stick to his original idea and cast him off in the little jolly-boat or the worm-eaten cutter, Bligh would have started sinking before he reached Tofoa and the sharks would have taken over the story.

Even so, eighteen men had to squeeze into a ten-seater boat, among the compasses, carpenter's box, the coconuts and breadfruit and the barrels of water, rum and wine. After a few hours, discomfort turned to aching pain, and a system had to be devised or else they'd go mad. First Fryer took the tiller, then passed it on to someone else and swapped seats. At the same time Bligh divided everyone into watches of six people. All the while the others moved about, two men would be stretched out under the seats, trying to breathe some life back into their cramped bodies. The boat sailed through rough and smooth seas, wobbling its way across the Pacific as the men inched their way around into new positions. The transom bar—the cross-bar on the stern the tiller rested on—was a mere eight inches above the water-line, meaning the smallest ruffle of waves splashed in. The launch had to be baled out constantly, and a certain balance kept to prevent the stern sliding under. Every second of the voyage someone had to be awake in case a wave pitched the boat up and sank it.

Most of the Midshipmen and Able Seamen had stayed on the *Bounty*. Almost everyone cast off had particular training and experience. Thomas Ledward the surgeon, David Nelson the botanist, William Peckover the gunner, William Cole the boatswain, William Purcell the carpenter, Lawrence LeBogue the sailmaker, John Smith and Thomas Hall the cooks, Robert Lamb the butcher, John Samuel the clerk—all the skill the voyage possessed.

Throwing the good men off the ship was Christian's great mistake, and when the *Bounty* caught fire and burned up at Pitcairn Island and the mutineers eventually turned on each other in drunken savagery, it was a foreseeable outcome for men who had sought Paradise on earth but had wilfully rejected those with the skills needed to attain it.

Bligh was not the only one on the longboat with navigation skills. Fryer and William Cole had them, and quite likely he could have trusted William Peckover, William Elphinston and Peter Linkletter with the instruments. Such men understood what was involved in reaching Timor, and that Bligh's leadership was necessary if they were to succeed. This was an important ingredient in holding them together in the weeks to come.

During the first few days the Captain tried to keep the crew's spirits up by telling them what they could expect when they reached New Holland and passed by New Guinea. Not that he had much of an idea himself. From what he'd read and from what he'd been told, the people on the coast of New Guinea were unrepentant savages. They painted themselves up to look like ghosts and lived in a perpetual state of war. He'd read

Dutch accounts of warriors adorning themselves with the bones of their enemies and of spectacular and terrifying rituals around great bonfires. The more colourful his descriptions became the more he realized how unpleasant the men found them. So soon after John Norton's death they weren't sure they'd be spared the same fate, and, as fearless as they could be in battle against the French or other Europeans, they were frightened of cultures they couldn't understand. It was horrible to imagine your body being dragged into the depths of the jungle and butchered. Bligh had hoped they'd find some amusement in his stories but some of them asked him instead to change the topic.

Through sheets of stinging rain and vomitous swells they caught glimpses of land—small, flat islands Bligh knew from Cook's journals to be the outlying Feejeeans. If the people of Tongatabu, Otaheite and the Sandwiches were mercurial and unpredictable by reputation, the Feejeeans were at least consistent. They were known to kill and eat trespassers without exception.

One hundred and thirty-seven years earlier, Abel Tasman had entered the archipelago, sketched and named about twenty islands—most of which turned out to be mountains on Vanua Levu—then headed north and swung back to Batavia. Barely touched by this intrusion, the islands remained unknown until 1774, when on his second voyage Cook mapped Turtle Island before sailing south-east for the Friendlys. When he sat down to banquets of roasted pig and breadfruit with Chief Paulaho he was also fed all manner of tales about how repulsive the Feejeeans were.

So Bligh was mindful that the inhabitants of these islands had a dangerous reputation. On the 7th of May, just six days after Norton had been killed, two canoes slid out from an island and chased the launch. Pausing long enough to note that the craft were similar in construction to those he'd seen in the Friendlys, Bligh ordered his men to heave away at the oars.

When he had his chance a few months later, Fryer would recall this as a scene of panic and anger: the Captain at the tiller bellowing his lungs out and Lawrence LeBogue retorting with equal passion that he, at least, was ready to fight while others cowered, terrified that the Captain's mad helmsmanship would see them all overboard. But by that time Fryer was sick with hatred and the slightest change in Bligh's tone had passed into his memory as a screaming rage. For their pursuers the scene must have been absurd— eighteen grown men shouting and cursing in a tiny boat as they splashed frantically towards the empty sea. Eventually the Europeans shook off the canoes, never to know if the Feejeeans were hungry or merely curious.

Now William Bligh settled down to his life's ambition. He was soaked and hungry, the cuts from the Tongan stones had begun to fester and he was in a foul mood, but he was also surrounded by islands crying out to be charted. Maps, figures, instruments and books were essential to the existence of those in the boat.

Thomas Hayward's little signal book contained all

the advice pertinent to a conscientious Midshipman—
five fathoms a blue flag, ten fathoms a white flag,
fifteen fathoms a red flag ... A jack at the main-
topgallant-masthead is a signal for the boats away to
repair on board ... No more than one man is to quit the
boat at a time in any place where there may be
Indians—advice to learn off by heart so you could
watch your superiors break all the rules then figure out
for yourself why. That is called learning. Small enough
to fit in a man's coat pocket, water-stained pages made
of cotton rag, it was a useless luxury for an oaf like
Hayward who'd spent most of the voyage asleep on the
sacks of grain. But for a man driven to survive the high
seas it was a lifeline. Weaker men, brighter men
perhaps, might use the blank pages to inscribe
thoughts—a diary of their descent into everlasting
gloom. Words were fine for the folks back home but a
man who really knew the sea and how to live by it
would fill his book with figures—latitude and longitude, log-lines, compass points, wind directions—and
each figure represented progress, distance made, one
step closer to the home-fires. Words were abstractions,
numbers real, and no poet or diarist could look upon his
scribblings and say with the same self-confidence: here
is the clear proof I am alive and I am going to keep on
living.

Ten leagues away an island dominating the others
around it shimmered through the haze on the horizon.
Instinctively Bligh steered the boat towards it. The
low, sandy atolls had given way to thick, green
mountains rising like monuments above the sea, and as
they sailed through a passage he busied himself with

the sextant and the book of tables, calculating his position and making a hasty sketch of the islands in the notebook, hunched over to protect it from the sea-water.

Here and there ribbons of smoke rose above the treetops and they caught snatches of drumbeats or hammering bouncing faintly across the water. It was a struggle to keep the boat far enough away from land to remain hidden, and he wasn't just fighting the currents or the wind. A devil inside was telling him to put his faith in human goodness and make for shore. Had not a mere forty-four men just sailed into Otaheite and spent six happy months cultivating breadfruit? There were thousands of Indians on that island and had they wanted to they could have overwhelmed the English-men in a matter of minutes. And even the warriors at Tofoa. What, apart from human reason, had stopped them from killing all the castaways on the beach? And these were rich, black-soiled islands. You could practi-cally smell the fertility bursting out from the moun-tain-sides. A few days here could see them refreshed, their wounds healed and ready to set sail once again . . . cannibals. Like every other white man who'd visited these parts he'd never actually seen anyone out here eating human flesh. He'd always believed the stories because they added a certain shiver to the whole adventure, and it gave the people a barbarity consistent with their nakedness. And so, remembering the fate of poor John Norton, he decided not to land.

He barked at Robert Lamb to hold the tiller while he completed his calculations. Nothing was to distract him from the important work of mapping these so far

uncharted waters, not even a devil calling him to shore
. . . One day an English or a French frigate might well
find eighteen stark white skeletons drifting aimlessly
in waters far away from here, but they'd find the
notebook too and they'd remember William Bligh—
explorer, discoverer and man of the King's Royal Navy
to the very end.

* * *

THREE YEARS LATER Bligh was to stand on the deck of
the *Providence*, on his second (successful) breadfruit
mission, looking out at this same island, the gold
buttons on his blue coat shining in the white palms of
a black man. This fellow had arrived by canoe with
three companions that morning, trading spears for
hatchets. Small and very dark, more like some of the
African slaves Bligh had encountered in Jamaica than
the Otaheiteans, his hair was plaited with a foul-
smelling grease and his ear-lobes hung obscenely low,
an enormous hole in each one large enough to hang a
brick by a stout rope if he wanted. Like the others he
had a couple of fingers cut off, and one had to wonder
what that meant. Did it mark some rite of passage into
manhood? Could it have something to do with fat
Paulaho's claim years ago that the best parts of a man
to eat were his fingers and they were always reserved
for the chief?

On the whole these people appeared more primitive,
meaner and more cunning in their gestures than the
Otaheiteans—as though they could cheerfully eat
another person—yet stroking the buttons and giggling,

his eyes wide and soft as he looked up to the white man, this Indian possessed such a childish innocence it was possible to believe he'd be offended at eating meat of any description.

Then Bligh thought back to the last time he'd come through here, and smiled to himself at the notion they could well have landed the launch and rested comfortably for a few days. What had come afterwards had been so awful, so horrific, it had overshadowed all his memories of these islands. Somehow, he recalled, they'd all been fit and in good spirits at this stage of the journey.

Someone on the *Providence* asked the Feejeeans about Tongatabu and they became excited, pointing in the precise direction of that island. One of them slapped his buttocks and the others fell about laughing—an obscene joke at the expense of the Tonga-tabuans—then the trading started up again in earnest.

Walking away to speak with his Master, Bligh asked that the figures for longitude be checked once again. It was of critical importance that they be as exact as possible. With every voyage now new islands were being discovered and it was imperative that everyone understand these were Bligh's Islands—not the Solomons or the New Hebrides as some might think. There could be no mistake. The Master had to understand that.

Bligh's Islands . . . a vision of his daughters walking into the great oak and marble hall of the Admiralty Office and staring up at a vast engraved map of the Pacific . . . there, far out in the middle of nowhere, were Bligh's Islands, close to Banks' Islands, and not so far from Cook's Islands . . . Cook, Banks, Bligh—Cook the Father, Bligh the Son and Banks the Holy Ghost, the great Trinity of Pacific exploration. He could see his girls as clearly as if they were standing beside him. They'd gaze up in awe, their eyes shining with wonder at an ocean too enormous for them possibly to understand the magnificence of their father's achievement, unable to find where Otaheite was, and they'd look way below the Equator for the Sandwich Isles, but they'd know exactly where Bligh's Islands were, and the men passing by—hardened old warhorses and thin-lipped admirals—would pause to smile indulgently. 'Oh, so you're *his* daughters, are you?'

The Master gave him a set of numbers and he compared them to some written down in the log . . . a couple of degrees out longways but that was to be expected and it would make no difference. He made another entry.

He had named every island around here now, including the big one, and he knew he was the first European to do so . . . the big one was Z because he'd charted it after Y Island. In a gesture that revealed the extraordinary vivacity of his imagination he'd gone all the way through from A at the perimeter of the archipelago and now he had to ask himself what came after Z. It wasn't simple for one could not afford to be at all confusing. A lesser mind might interpret some false relationship between A and B or assume the errors in their calculations were actually William Bligh's. Better perhaps to give them a compass point and a number—ENE1, SSW2?

The *Providence* sailed from Feejee leaving not so

much as a Harriet, an Elizabeth or a Maria Island behind, let alone the conventional names of patrons, government figures or heads of state. X, Y and Z they would be.

Cook and Banks, along with a number of individuals whose connections with the Pacific were distinctly tenuous, would be memorialized for a long time in the names of islands and archipelagos, but 'Bligh's Islands' never caught on. People simply used the exotic and sensible 'Feejee'. Like 'Otaheite' the word evoked more than any captain, king or prime minister's name could ever hope to. Bligh would be immortalized for many things, but never as one of the great explorers of the Pacific.

* * *

Taking a coconut and holding it firmly against the side of the boat, Bligh split it in half with one blow and moved quickly to stop the juice spilling. With an old tin teaspoon he'd found in the carpenter's box he gave each of the men a sip, himself last, then scooped out the flesh with the sword blade and handed that around. Left with just the brown shell, he crossed a long piece of twine around both halves and tied it so they sat at each end, then he took a piece of dowling from the chest and a few musket balls he'd found in his pocket and presented everyone with a set of scales. Twenty-five balls equalled one pound, or sixteen ounces, and from here on their ration of pork and of bread would equal one musket ball—not much more than a sniff really.

Nobody else shared his enthusiasm for the invention.

Taking another coconut shell and some more twine he made a log-line, tossed it out near the stempost and counted the seconds till the boat had passed it, then one by one he took the others through—'One-and a-two-and a-three'—until he was satisfied they could count a reasonably accurate second.

When Europeans first left the safety of the Atlantic coast in the early fifteenth century and reached out nervously for the unknown, they knew that measuring the speed of their ships was imperative if they wanted to return home. Without even rudimentary calculations there was nothing to stop them sailing too far out one way and becoming lost on the homeward leg, or not going far enough and, on their return, smashing their ships at night upon rocky coasts they had expected to encounter several days later.

It was not especially difficult to work out their speed and the simplest method was to toss a log overboard and count how long it took for the ship to pass by. From these first, crude experiments the procedure developed into one where the log (or any sizeable piece of wood) was tied to a rope which was fed out to measure the distance the ship then travelled from the (theoretically) stationary piece of wood. Knots were tied in the rope to increase the accuracy of the measurement so that two new words—'log' and 'knot'—entered the language of the sea. So early navigators had the skills and implements to make intelligent guesses, and the only real improvement to the system had been the invention of the chronometer.

Without one Bligh and his men were no worse off than most sailors through history.

Of course it's pointless if you don't know where you're going—if you're adrift in the open sea without any idea what landfalls lie ahead or behind. Why then would you need to know how fast you're travelling? But Bligh had a destination. Again, he depended upon that map he kept inside his head. He had spent hours at a time poring over Cook's charts and memorizing the latitude positions of coastal landmarks, albeit aware that even the Great Man's efforts involved guesswork and were bound to have errors of unknowable proportions. Bligh's talent, his genius even, involved taking this long education and transforming it into an instinctive feel for the dimensions of the Earth, as if he could see this speck of a boat bobbing on the ocean, and calculate where exactly on the still mysterious globe it was.

'If it takes four seconds to pass a twenty-three foot boat, at what rate of knots are we travelling?'

Silence. Only the mainsail flapping damply in the breeze.

'Tinkler?'

'How should I know?'

'Mr Elphinston?'

'Six, Captain.'

'How did you come by that figure?'

'I guessed it.'

'It isn't horribly wrong. I say we're travelling four knots with a good wind, otherwise two.'

No one could disagree.

'Let's assume it is four thousand miles to Timor . . .

How long will it take? . . . Mr Smith?'

'About forty-one days, Captain.'

'How can you be so sure?'

'That is one thousand hours divided by twenty-four, give or take.'

'You show a penchant for mathematics I never would have guessed at. So tell us, Smith; how much coconut can each man have a day?'

'I don't know.'

'Work it out, man, work it out.' His cheerfulness was strained and seemed to drift off with the breeze. If anyone smiled it was tightly, politely.

'A very small amount?'

'D'you see this cut on my chin where the Indian's stone scored? It still aches. If it was to become infected tonight so that by tomorrow I was no good but to feed the fishes, how long would you lot last? . . . No answer, eh? Well, I don't know who of you I'd want handing out the rations. It would be the choice between a quick death and a slightly quicker one.'

'Which is better any day than a slow one.'

'True, Mr Ledward, but death requires its own dignity and I'd hate to think of you lot cleaning out the larder in a few minutes then going mad with fear. That happens. If you do die after me, do it with style. Toss me off if I start to smell, hoist the flag then lie down quietly. Be gentlemen in your most important hour.'

Nobody laughed. He alone seemed to think they had a fair chance of any other fate.

'I'm going to teach you boys a few tricks of navigation so if something does happen one or two of you should acquit yourselves well enough to reach

Timor. Can you read the heavens, Mr Samuel? No? You won't be much help to yourself if you're all alone out here, will you? . . . By my calculation we are 16.04 degrees south—which is lucky for you lot.'

At sixteen degrees south the intersections between lines of longitude and latitude were still square enough not to be significantly influenced by the curvature of the globe. To an experienced cartographer the world in these regions looked and behaved very much like it did on a Mercator projection—the lines were straight, the earth was flat. It meant plotting a course in a square rather than a distended rhomboid as would happen further south—'plane sailing' as it was known best. Because they were travelling due west, Bligh knew that they would inevitably hit the coast of New Holland so long as they kept within the same latitudes. However much people would later flatter him for his brilliance as a navigator, this was child's play. It was only because the distance was so vast they would imagine the feat was equal in its proportions. The real challenge would come when they had to negotiate a poorly-charted coast inside the Barrier Reef and into the Torres Strait. Peckover knew from his voyage on the *Endeavour* that their way would be littered with islands, reefs and dangerous shoals.

Had Bligh had the generosity he might have admitted that navigation on this voyage would have been basic work for John Fryer too. But rejection and embitterment had reinforced in Bligh a sense of his own specialized worth. A good navigator had to know his trigonometry as well as any decent mathematician, and he needed to be able to visualize the way ahead with nothing to go on but a few abstract figures. In a part of the world which the best maps showed as little more than a few broken lines, a navigator had to *feel* where those lines joined up. He had to be able to predict so that all his expectations were met by what lay just over the horizon. Fryer was useful—he could take charge of one of the watches and steer the boat safely through the night—but he lacked the brilliance, the vision . . .

Holding the sextant (a Ramsden ten-inch of finely polished brass: the very best on the market) up high, Bligh explained how it worked. The navigator looked through the small eyepiece at the horizon then found a stationary celestial body, such as the sun, and, swinging the index arm so its image was caught by the small mirror at the top of the instrument, he then moved the index arm until the sun appeared to sit on the horizon. The angle on the curved scale at the base of the sextant was the same as the elevation of the sun. It was so elegantly simple. All one had to do then was find the meridian according to the book of tables, then calculate latitude with a straightforward trigonometric equation.

Immediately Bligh set about revealing to the others the secrets of navigation, he became lost in the figures, calculating the transverse lines or angle of hypotenuse from his sextant reading and expecting them to follow each step as though they already knew it well. They tried, afraid this was the very stuff that would save their lives, but most of it went over their heads.

One by one each of the men (except Fryer, who found Bligh's humour dull and his instructions unnecessary) went through the process, just as they'd done with the log-line, until the Captain decided they could at least make the sextant work.

Though he wanted to put the fear of God into all and get them thinking he might very well keel over before the next sunrise, in his heart he knew there'd be plenty of time to polish up their navigation skills. He could probably work it out to the very minute if he could be bothered, but at a stab he gave them another two months before they'd see a white face again—if they made it.

* * *

THE MOON PIERCES the great curtain of clouds above, its pallid, vaporous light scattered so weakly it barely falls upon the water at all. A delicate mist of rain, fine enough gently to saturate them passes on and in its place large drops spit down. A body stirs, a restless dream, a thick and incoherent Orkney accent mumbling the snatch of a plea to be left alone . . .

John Fryer takes his hand from the tiller and leans back, letting the raindrops splash on to his face. Stretching one leg out, feeling for resistance from other bodies, he finds a space and lets the leg extend until someone shifts uncomfortably and traps it against the seat. Slowly, so he won't disturb anyone, he withdraws, enjoying every inch of movement he can give the limb. His legs feel dead, as if below the knees he had pieces of flesh stitched on to his body after the rest of it was born, and day by day he can feel the death creeping up, spreading like a cancer.

In the darkness a head jerks up and stares wildly

around before collapsing again. It is the Captain, trapped in the worst dream of all, where for a cruel moment he is back on dry land, among the green fields of England and under a warm sun.

Fryer studies that milk-white face and feels his weariness turn brittle with resentment. Not once during the navigation lesson did Bligh look at him, ask his advice or listen to his suggestions. The Captain may well have decided he didn't exist. When Bligh had made a small error in his calculations and he had spoken up to point out the Captain should have said 10.30 degrees south instead of 10.40, he had been wilfully ignored and the mistake corrected as though Bligh was just about to do it anyway. Even Peckover, not so hot at navigation, had been allowed to put his tuppence-worth in. When they'd talked about the Torres Strait, how dangerous it was with islands suddenly appearing out of nowhere and sandbars lying like crocodiles just below the surface, it was as if they were the only two men among the lot who'd done any proper sailing. They spoke as though everyone else was a novice, even though Bligh hadn't actually seen the Torres Strait yet.

As for Nelson! What a damned botanist knew about navigation was anyone's guess, but he was Bligh's friend—his 'best' friend—and even the most idiotic question from 'David' was answered with proper respect, as if it was refreshing to have someone brighter than the average imbecile on board.

Of course the Captain had been very careful not to be seen to be deliberately ignoring Fryer. He'd been very measured and quick to throw his questions about so there were no pauses he could interrupt. Even the lad Tinkler didn't appear to notice there was a problem. That was all part of the Captain's game. He wouldn't rub it in, he wouldn't gloat—at least not openly—and he'd leave himself the opportunity to appear quite innocent should he be challenged. Somewhere else, in other circumstances, he would have answered the Captain's smugness with a good smack in the chops. Here, for the time being anyway, he had to sit patiently and stew a bit. Very well, an opportunity would come.

There'd been a few before. There'd been one instance when he had it all over William Bligh. After weeks battling the storms of the Southern Ocean the *Bounty* had arrived at Adventure Bay. No Europeans had been there since the *Resolution* eleven years earlier and it was still the same strange and pristine forest of giants. Out of the trunks of trees they'd cut down for planking back then they found saplings sprouting twenty-five feet high, and Nelson measured one tree and found its girth was thirty-three feet in diameter. Among this primal exuberance they discovered a date: *AD 1773*, carved into a trunk, and could only guess at how it came to be there.

From the ship the men pulled up rock cod and along the shore they threw out nets and hauled in flathead, flounder and crabs. Mussels encrusted the rocks and the sailors ate them till they turned green. Others hunted the birds, which Bligh sketched, and inside the forest apple, plum, orange, peach, lemon, apricot, pumpkin, pear and cherry seeds were planted.

One morning as he rowed to shore Bligh heard a

sound like a cackling of geese and twenty natives emerged from the bush. Their chests studded with cicatrices, the men had painted their bodies with a dark ash or ochre so that they appeared unearthly. Once the Captain had somewhat timorously thrown trinkets to them a discussion—such as it could be—was held on the beach. When Cook had been here he'd met a hunchback who'd appeared to compensate for his deformity with extravagant gestures while he spoke. The same man now stood before Bligh, throwing his arms about and pointing out to sea while the Englishmen smiled blandly, unsure of how to respond once the beads and copper nails had been distributed.

The good Lord himself could not have directed the *Bounty* to a more pleasant spot for refreshment before she entered the Pacific. The crew, tired of the rough seas and the diet of pumpkin, salted pork, soup and sauerkraut, filled their lungs with the bracing air and found work far more agreeable beneath the high forest canopy than under sail. Only William Purcell the carpenter had a problem. There was, as John Fryer agreed, a matter of principle at stake.

The ship's carpenter was legally a Warrant Officer with the added proviso that he signed on with his own tools. According to Royal Navy regulations he couldn't be flogged, he could only be confined to quarters, and, by propriety, the Captain could not have full command over his tools or his space. On long expeditions away from Mother England authority could be nebulous and it was usual for a ship to carry a number of marines to clarify the situation, with force if required. On the *Bounty* the only real protection between Bligh and his

Warrant Officers was common sense, and the prospect that one day the ship would return home and reports would be submitted.

William Purcell decided the Captain's request that he go off and *labour* with the wood-cutting crew was an affront both to his rank and his trade. It didn't take long to find a sympathetic ear.

'Quite right,' the Master nodded. 'Give him an inch and he'll take a mile. Next he'd have us washing the slops.'

Of course, under *normal* circumstances the carpenter might have been less belligerent, but with Fryer apparently on his side there was no one to reinforce the Captain's position over him and, with a crew of only forty-five, a carpenter was too valuable to lock up for several months. If he chose to ignore orders, what could Bligh do about it?

The Captain ordered him to remain on board under Mr Fryer's guard, carting water down to the hold. Two days later he discovered Purcell had done nothing of the sort and a confrontation between the three of them took place in the storeroom. Among barrels of strong-smelling pickled cabbage and malt Fryer pleaded his innocence. He could not order another Warrant Officer about—what power did he have?—and if Mr Purcell refused to do labouring work there wasn't a lot he could do about it. It wasn't his fault. It was regulations.

Bligh was livid. His cheeks flushed, his lip trembling, he called Purcell a poltroon, a scug, an unmanly slob and a gutless scrimshanker and swore that once back in England the carpenter would pay with a court-martial so swift and vicious he'd be swinging from a Newgate gibbet before the judge's last words were out.

In the meantime, Purcell shrugged, the Captain should find someone else to carry the water and chop down trees. He was a carpenter, not a damn blacka-moor and he wasn't here to do another's job.

'Damn your eyes!' Bligh shook with constricted rage. However high the carpenter's principles might be, his were to live by the letter of the law, whatever the consequences. Here, as far away from England as he could ever expect to be, the law might just as well have been written up in the language of the Hottentots for all the good it served him. His response to Purcell was as reckless as it was predictable.

He took written evidence from Fryer and Purcell and made the public order that the carpenter was to be denied food, drink or clean clothes until he returned to work. There and then Purcell picked up a small barrel and went off to have it filled with water. That was all you had to do to keep the Captain in tow. All his posturing, his insults, his invocations of British Justice, were hogwash out here. A strong Captain would have picked up the cat, let loose and bugger the regulations. A bad Captain cowered behind them. If he looked silly protesting about the carpenter in front of the crew he'd look pathetic in two or three years time (or whenever they got back home) presenting to the Admiralty a list of offenders he'd been unable to control. Who would take him seriously? Especially when it was clear the Warrant Officers had humiliated him within the very confines of the law he was so adamant in upholding?

A small wave broke over the stern of the launch,

snapping the Master out of his reverie. Automatically he reached for a coconut shell and began baling the water out from around his boots. Up by the stempost Robert Lamb heard him swear and passed down a pail via George Simpson. The men spoke quietly, Fryer cursing the bastard who had got them into this mess.

There was a very simple rule in his book. A man was a leader only as long as he could lead. Call him ruthless, but to be anything other than pragmatic about leadership was dangerous, especially out here. While the *Bounty* was being fitted out and victualled, and at Spithead before they sailed, William Bligh had been all hearty jokes and his sense of adventure had been infectious, but no sooner had they sailed past the Needles than the façade cracked like Venice glass. This expedition had been a misery under the captaincy of a man who made mistake after mistake and in the process exposed his crew to every pain and discomfort they could endure, and the Master felt no bitterness towards Christian and the others for turning back to Otaheite. Well, but for bitterness that he hadn't been included. He could imagine the scene now—their bellies full of pigmeat and sugarcane, the scent of hibiscus catching their nostrils as a honey-coloured nymphet pressed her wet little body up against theirs.

In the afternoon Bligh took out his scales and gave each man a half-ounce of pork and a scrap of bread. The taste had scarcely touched their mouths before the morsel of meat was gone. The bread was stale, dusted with a fine web of mould.

These small rations did nothing for hunger except

aggravate it. And Bligh was so finicky with the distribution. He could tell now without trying how small a cube of pork had to be to measure up to a musket ball but he would still weigh each one, and if the launch hit a rough patch or a good breeze disturbed his arm he'd begin again. They were to get half an ounce, no more no less, and did it really need half an hour to divide up such pathetically tiny rations? The man who received his portion first might be chewing his knuckle in quiet frustration by the time the last (Bligh himself) was served but he'd have no cause to complain that someone was getting more than him. And the Captain was deaf when the men begged for just a scrap more.

Ever since leaving Bligh's Islands they'd had nothing but foul weather. There were days when the rain never let up for a second but poured down, drenching the men and swamping the boat. As fast as they baled the launch filled up. The bread was spoiled and the meat turned bad. And these were the good days. On the evening of the 10th of May black clouds built up above them and the lightning forked down. That night and for the next two days they endured the tail of a cyclone still fierce enough to suck them up to the crests of great waves then slam them down to the base. On the night of the eleventh they worked through until the morning, terrified by the screaming wind and the waves driving the small boat helplessly forward. A few days earlier Bligh and LeBogue had rigged up a couple of ropes to secure the masts, and stitched a spare strip of canvas around the sides of the boat to protect them from the weather. The masts didn't break and they were given a little refuge from the wind but they couldn't escape from the rain or the cold and they had no control over the launch's direction. When the storms abated on the morning of the twelfth, the wind and rain didn't cease but merely slackened. They had to put up with drizzle now. Not so dramatic but just as pernicious in the misery it dealt out.

Under a grey sky and on the surface of a rolling sea Bligh doled out a teaspoon of rum and a piece of bread to each man. Their faces were ashen—exhausted from two sleepless nights and starved for something more than a few crumbs or a sniff of spirit. Some of the men were complaining that though they felt an intense urge to crap, nothing was happening. Their bodies were seizing up and Bligh was worried. He could navigate the launch, he could take it through the most ferocious storms, but he could do nothing if they fell ill, and neither, it seemed, could Mr Ledward without his potions and salves. The thought of them dying slowly from scurvy, starvation or the relentless effects of the weather appalled Bligh. It was a horrid, lonely and Godless death, and it would be a personal failure. He had no control over the weather and if it chose to send up a wave which smashed the launch to splinters there was naught he could about that, but he should be able to save the men from scurvy and starvation. He was in charge of the food, he dispensed it, he was responsible for their health.

Thomas Hall begged for just a scrap more meat. His limbs were dead as fence-posts and colic twisted his guts into knots. He was not far, he was certain, from his final breath.

The Captain smiled weakly. He would not have vowed to sail to Timor if it had not been possible, and to do it he could not soften his stand on the rations. If he did, he knew they'd gorge themselves on the pork, the rum and the breadfruit and death would be a formality. Surely in those eyes full of hunger and pleading there was also a flicker of common sense, enough to remember the promises they'd made just off Tofoa, and why they'd made them.

But the *shivering*. Surely the Captain could feel it himself and know there was a cold touch to the wind and it *did* ruffle their skin, but there was also a cold *inside*, that came from the very marrow in the bones and it felt sometimes as if the shiver was the body's one last effort before it gave up the ghost. How wrong to die this way when there was a barrel of rum and a sack of pork on hand—just the very things to light the spark in the old bones once more. What righteous stand could the Captain take if he didn't give them precious sustenance in the proper amounts?

In the evening he gave them a piece of stale bread and half a tin cup of water. Their resignation to an even more tasteless and unsatisfying meal than they may have otherwise expected couldn't disguise the gloom in their eyes and those ash-grey faces.

One problem he could help them with concerned the constant saturation of their clothes by the rain. Not only was it uncomfortable, but it was dangerous—the source of deep chills that could very well kill them with pneumonia if the showers didn't let up. His solution was to make them strip off, soak their clothes in sea-water, wring them out and put them back on. It was an old trick, of the type not found in manuals but passed on through the folklore of the sea. Salt water evaporates faster than fresh, so clothes soaked in it dry faster. With what precious sunlight there was they might enjoy an hour or so a day of dry warmth and it might save their lives.

Soaking clothes in sea-water and wringing them out was the one piece of advice William Bligh would pass on for anyone who might find themselves adrift on a boat in the middle of nowhere. He would have nothing to say about his methods with the rations, save that the others would have died without him.

In the morning a few small birds dived about the waves nearby and in the afternoon a small green fruit from the fish poison tree bobbed alongside the boat. Frigate-birds wheeled in the sky above and a dim-looking booby perched on the mast-head. The following dawn they saw the high blue smudge of distant mountains and Bligh realized they were at the northern edge of the New Hebrides. No decent explorer of the South Seas could ignore their cursed history of mutiny and madness.

In 1605 Pedro Fernandes de Quiros had sailed west from Peru in search of Terra Australis. Sick, crazed and inflamed with Christian passion, he found a large island which he declared to be the Great South Land and named it *Tierra Austrialis del Espiritu Santo*; the Southern Land of the Holy Ghost. By then his crew were terrified as much by their Captain's behaviour as by the small, ferocious inhabitants out on the rim of the known world and they mutinied. His lieutenant, Luis Vaez de Torres, sailed on to penetrate the straits between Australia and New Guinea while Quiros returned to Spain—to hospitals, madhouses, prison and his endless petitions to return.

The havoc wreaked upon the minds and bodies of Spanish and Portuguese explorers out here had become legendary. Before Quiros, his former Captain Mendaña de Niera had searched for the fabled Ophir and gone mad while his crew murdered one another on the nearby Solomons, and before them Magellan and his ships managed to cross the Pacific without seeing a single island before the Philippines, dying in spades from starvation and scurvy in the process. The great Spanish and Portuguese visions of King Solomon's gold and fabulous lost continents foundered out here, cut down by the sheer expanse of the ocean.

But it wasn't the threat of madness or starvation that gave William Bligh so much anguish—not right now. It was the prospect of having to sail past so many islands bursting with food and relief for their long-suffering limbs. Tofoa and John Norton's death still haunted him. Yet the men were desperate, due to their hunger, the miserable rations, the cold and the constant, drumming rain. The Siren sight of smoke rising through the treetops teased them with thoughts of warm fires and tormented their appetites, but the Captain was steadfast. They were lucky to have made it this far without drowning and he wasn't prepared to risk their good fortune in a confrontation with warriors and cannibals. Ignoring the protests, he ordered the helmsman to keep his head forward and everyone else their eyes down. It hurt, he knew, to slip past islands offering food and warmth as though they weren't there.

Bent forward, his coat wide open to shelter the precious pages, he sketched rapidly, his fingers shaking uncontrollably. The rest of his arm felt dead, his elbow as stiff as if it had seized up with rust, and he couldn't stretch it out without bolts of pain shooting up to his shoulder, but the pencil jumped about in a fever. He couldn't escape the phantom scent of pigmeat either. There were no cooking fires about to blow the smell over and none of the others appeared to be craving it, but pigmeat such as they'd tasted on Otaheite and New Amsterdam wafted about his nostrils while he drew—images of steaming piles of flesh served up on plantain leaves afflicted him as he tried to guess the shape of the island based on Hallet's readings off the sextant. Huge feasts squatting around bonfires, the faces in the firelight glistening with pork-grease as they crammed it into their mouths—so much meat they let big steaks drop into the sand to be fought over by the scrawny island dogs; steaks he could imagine now sliding down his throat like hot butter . . . his fingers throbbed as he clutched the pencil in his fist, trying his damnedest to keep a steady hand and not snap the lead as the launch rocked through the waves.

If Hallet had read the sextant correctly they were a little to the north of what Cook and Bougainville reckoned to be the New Hebrides, in which case this could be a whole new and uncharted archipelago. At the risk of offending the memory of the Great Man he would act as he would have done and treat it as a fresh discovery, and if he was wrong, let the men of the Admiralty prove it. He could see some of them now, perched up on their bench with their gaunt, leathery faces seemingly impervious to all human emotion. There would be a pregnant silence, a hesitant tension, before the bench of lords cleared their collective throats and one of them spoke up for the rest with a high, clipped and officious tone. He would find it 'exceedingly remarkable' that William Bligh had discovered so many new islands. 'This alone was worthy of merit, but, that he did so whilst suffering the most abominable hardships, the victim of a villainous mutiny cast off to die on the high seas, that he had, no less, persisted in serving Britain with diligence and courage above the call of duty, was something no promotion, medal or trophy could ever compensate. Human rewards are but tokens. The glory comes from on high.'

The small but privileged audience would gather round—Betsy's eyes moist with pride and his daughters blushing crimson as they curtsied—the back-slaps, the handshakes, the toasts; and there, mincing through the portico on some petty business of his own, James King, bemused by all the kerfuffle, the smile cracking that deathly face as before his peers he has no way out but to extend his hand in a frozen, choked congratulation.

These should be called Banks' Islands, after the patron of the expedition. None of them looked as big as the best the Friendlys had to offer, but there were some good harbours butting up to the beaches and the green hills promised sanctuary and sustenance. The inhabitants, whoever they were, obviously lacked the joyful hedonism of the Otaheiteans, but these could be useful outposts for the future, when all the tribulations of the pioneers had faded from popular memory and the Jack fluttered triumphant all the way to the shores of Peru. It would be politic, the right thing, to acknowledge Sir Joseph here.

To larboard the clouds were piling up again, becoming dense and black on the horizon before rolling out to cover the rest of the sky. One of Mother Carey's chickens—a sure sign of terrible storms on the rise—circled the boat before beating its wings and gliding away to some distant, unknown shelter. Without waiting for the Captain's orders, Fryer and Elphinston reefed the sails and LeBogue belayed the shrouds. A fork of lightning crackled above and a faint residue of thunder was heard from behind.

That night the heavens ripped apart. The rain hammered down with the sting of a whip as the sea boiled furiously and the wind kicked the launch about as if it was paper. Under a black, roaring sky the men cowered and baled frantically, almost helpless, clinging on for dear life as the boat skimmed the crest of the swell then crashed to its base, swept up again and hurtled irresistibly towards a shuddering collision between wind and water.

At the mercy of the elements, Bligh could do little but wait for the sky to clear. Until then he had no idea in which direction the tempest sent them spinning, and things were hopeless while he could not see the sun or the moon. But it wouldn't let up. Dawn came and the only change was a lightening of the sky, enough to reveal the grey exhaustion in the men, and a faint, yellow ball pulsing fitfully through the clouds. The rain was unrelenting and the sea still raged without restraint. With a shaking hand he gave each man a spoonful of rum and urged them to keep baling.

The sails popped in a sudden gust and the boat lurched forward as a white water-spout twisted like a serpent towards them, brushing past and dissolving into mist. Once again the men stripped down and wrung out their clothes, scooped the water out from around their shins and tossed it out. He gave each of them a scrap of pork, then tried to take the best reading he could from a barely visible sun and a rolling, unsteady horizon. By his estimations they had travelled nearly a hundred miles since Tofoa, sucked along by the force of the gales.

As the sun began its decline the wind picked up and chilled the rain. Once more the clouds appeared to cram into the sky until they turned black to bursting point and the swell rose to throw the launch around. In a desperate weariness Bligh ordered everyone to keep baling—keep baling and keep the sun on the starboard side.

The words hardly made sense tumbling out of his mouth. His jaw ached—not from talking but from the fatigue and the cold that crept like a sickness through his bones. He turned, dark-eyed and shivering, to the man sitting next to him—Nelson—and realized his skin was blotched with faint bruises and his nostrils caked with blood and salt. He was looking towards the bow of the launch, eyes glistening with something impenetrable but haunted, as though entranced by some misdeed long buried in his memory. As the wind picked up once more the botanist bowed his head and mumbled incoherently.

Bligh wouldn't dare admit to so much as an atom of sentimentality in these conditions, but to look at David Nelson—to see that good man's hollow, blood-caked face, all his wit and intelligence lost under an untidy beard—it made him sick with pity. His duty towards some of the men on this launch went beyond that of a Captain to his crew. It became personal; a matter of friendship.

A hand reached towards the Captain. John Hallet begged pitiably for a piece of bread. 'Bread. That's all. Not pork.' Little more than a whisper, a voice so weak and plaintive, like a child's, and everything said with what life he could find in his eyes. Bligh shook his head. A good performance, but they'd made a deal and it was a shameful weakness to go back on it.

Another voice, from behind the Captain, joined Hallet's, and someone else croaked the question of what good pork would be to a boatload of corpses.

He remained resolute. The food was to last them until Timor. To give in now would make sure it was just that—a boatload of corpses.

And how then were they expected to find the strength to fight off another night of storms? It was cruelty itself. They were sick, they hadn't slept for days and they were starving. What monster would let his most loyal men endure a small part of what they had? Who could have looked at the faces around him and not felt moved by pity and fed them all? It was heartless to maintain the rationing.

'And it is gutless,' Bligh retorted to these arguments, 'to break it.' He turned away to signal there'd be no further discussion but he was surrounded by the faces and had to look down to his feet buried in the sludge at the bottom of the boat to avoid them.

Under encroaching darkness the waves crashed across the boat and the men, by now inured to the shock of water, kept baling with the same tired rhythm. The wind seemed to screech across the surface of the sea towards them as the boat heaved upwards and slammed down again and lightning split the sky. He leaned back to protect the box of bread with his body.

Surely the men knew it was because he cared that he kept the rationing so tight? Whatever the pain in their eyes, a spark of common sense must have surely told them it was his pledge to see them all survive that made him appear so ruthless. What they couldn't know, what he could never admit, was that although his pain and his hunger were his to suffer alone, each wretched face, each choked plea also hurt him. He wasn't a tyrant. He'd simply made that pledge and he would do everything possible to keep it. The rain came down with such force it drowned out the thunder and drove thinking from his mind.

It was one of the small ironies he had to consider that the weather was keeping them alive. Had they been sailing under a clear sky the blazing tropical sun would have already brought most of the men to a point close to death. With what small amount of water they had they would have soon dehydrated, withering in the heat, and nothing could have saved them. They would have drained themselves, throats parched, too weak to take readings, too exhausted to care, and the appeals to Bligh would not have been pathetic but murderous, for hunger might debilitate but thirst sends people mad. The rain saved them from that fate. It saved them from thirst. Their dangers were the shortage of food and— more insidious and much more likely—hypothermia.

In the 1780s the Royal Navy was one of the great beneficiaries from a medical establishment rubbing the sleep of superstition and the occult from its eyes. Sailors were ideal guinea pigs for theories and experiments. Not only was the Navy the backbone of Britain's international strength, it was also an inexhaustible source of new illnesses. Sailors lived in extremes. They left port full of life and returned six months later shattered by disease. They enjoyed months of good health among the icebergs and floes of the north, then docked at Plymouth and promptly died. Everything from syphilis to bubonic plague and the various poxes seemed to emanate from the harbour towns into the rest of England, and as the century drew to its close and the Empire consolidated, a young chap with his eye on high society might consider coming up with a cure for something as the smart way in.

Plenty tried, but their efforts were bewildered by poor knowledge and false assumptions. The greatest medical thinkers of the age believed the foul air steaming out of swamps was poisonous and the sick men coming back from Jamaica must have breathed in too much of it. If you wore the same set of clothes for too long you contracted typhoid, and if so many gentlemen from the better classes fell victim to tuberculosis or gout there must have been a connection with their delicate minds and breeding. Tougher types were struck down by dysentery—something swift and violent rather than slow and wasting. Around the time James Lind was demonstrating that oranges and lemons had a positive effect on scurvy, and Benjamin Jesty was beating smallpox by vaccinating his brave wife and children with cowpox, the moneyed folk were visiting the piss prophets. For an extravagant fee these Harley Street shysters would take a sample of their patient's urine, hold it up to the light, sniff it as though it were the finest chardonnay, dab a little of it on with their tongues, close their eyes and announce their diagnosis. The rich weren't the only ones being fleeced. Down among the masses, Mary Tofts made herself a small fortune miraculously giving birth to rabbits and magnetism could do everything from preventing baldness to contacting the dead. Whatever the scheme there'd be someone who thought it was sensible.

Medicine was changing, but not fast enough. Alongside the Spinning Jenny and Crompton's Mule, the Industrial Revolution gave us knife-grinder's phthisis, tailor's ankle and weaver's bottom. They were all maladies of science—of chemicals and other substances supposed to liberate the workers, or more precisely their bosses, from tediously low productivity levels. Milliners worked with mercury, rubbing it in their hands and breathing it in, and slowly lost their minds. The same thinking that imagined swamp gas killed sailors rationalized that lead must have curative properties, and it was prescribed alongside arsenic for venereal diseases. (Heavy metals do indeed have an effect upon syphilis, but only because they tend to kill everything they come into contact with.) James Lind's work on citrus fruit and scurvy was really only the reiteration of knowledge which the Spanish and Portuguese had discovered a century and a half earlier, but he had to fight to be heard above the cacophony drummed up by dreamers, conmen and quacks.

Most sailors of the Georgian Navy had a cocktail of diseases ticking away inside them. Syphilis—take it for granted—malaria, fluxes, typhoid, tropical fevers, not to mention a menagerie of parasites. They'd all been laid low at some stage of the job, from time in the equatorial colonies festering with bugs that could pass through a native like water but wipe out a whole shipload of white folk (most Europeans had never heard a mosquito's whine), from the wretched English tenements they dossed down in, where it really was life-threatening to breathe in the air, and from the brothels which did a roaring seaside trade in cheap comfort. 'One night with Venus and six months with Mercury' was how the saying went, and that was pretty well how people regarded it. You caught it, you took the cure, and the ebb and flow of daily life was scarcely interrupted. For the record, of the launch party, William Cole, William Purcell, Lawrence LeBogue, Robert Lamb and John Smith had all paid the standard fifteen shilling fee to Dr Huggan or Thomas Ledward while at Otaheite.

Disease might take people to the very point of death then vanish, leaving their vital organs permanently, invisibly damaged, or it might, like syphilis, lie dormant until the last, horrid months of their life. A real danger for Bligh and his men lay in the stress they put upon their organs. Poor diet or the constant cold seeping through to liver, kidneys and lungs badly corroded by tuberculosis could see an apparently healthy individual take a turn for the worse and expire within the day. That much the Captain understood. He didn't know how to make a proper medical diagnosis but he had enough experience to know the signs of imminent death when they appeared.

As it happens, it takes a good six weeks before starvation kills, and Bligh's rations, pitiably mingy though they were, were enough to stretch to that. The human body can endure an astonishing amount. An adult, male, eighteenth-century sailor's needed about three thousand calories a day. When it isn't getting that, when in fact it starts expending that amount without consuming the same, rapid and serious weight loss sets in. Remarkably, it manages to draw sustenance from the darkest corners.

Fortunately the men had been healthy when they left the *Bounty*, much more so than when they had first boarded it. A sailor with time to kill between voyages wasted it within earshot of the piers. Unless he had family in other parts there'd be no reason to find lodgings elsewhere and so, waiting for a ship to be fitted out or touting for work, he took to liquor and women and had what fun he could find. Drinking, whoring, gambling—not much else in the way of amusement. Certainly he gave very little thought to eating except by way of quantity. For the most part it was meat—roasted or boiled—and potatoes, done the same. The tomato was still considered poisonous and the capsicum just a decorative exotic. Greens weren't edible unless you were sober. As a consequence a good number of the sailors embarking for a long voyage were already victims of the scurvy. They didn't realize it but that dry, flaky skin around their mouth or those bruised and weak fingernails were the first signs they wouldn't see home again. That was one of the reasons why the sickness was so mysterious and unpredictable—why one voyage might last several months without a single complaint while another had scarcely lost sight of land before the first symptoms became manifest.

But for the six months prior to being dumped in the launch, Bligh's men had been perhaps the best fed people in England's history. Breadfruit, coconut, plantains, yams, the small berries and tropical fruit Europeans were yet to name, and fish, pig and fowl-meat, all picked or freshly killed every day. Only fat, drunken, beetroot-faced surgeon Huggan had died at Otaheite and nothing could have saved him anyway. Everyone else thrived, and not only was their diet superb, they lived in a psychic idyll too. Out here, love was not only free, it was theirs to make of it what they wanted. Hardly surprising really that only a couple of the crewmen were recorded as taking in women as steady, Christian-style lovers. Why would the others when they could rise from the warm arms of one woman, leave the bed of palm fronds and beach sand and soon fall like ripe plums into another's? No commitments, no expectations, no jealousy—no guilt or deceit. For men whose kindest experiences with love had been in the gin-soaked bordellos of the port towns this was how God always intended it. Naturally the crewmen went native. They had their faces and bodies tattooed and they used Otaheitean words in everyday speech.

Six months of sun, love, good food and a little work now and then. When they left Otaheite they were in the best of health—mental and physical—and now it saved them from starvation and scurvy. Although Vitamin C doesn't hang around, the connective tissue breakdown that comes with a deficiency did not affect them before they reached Timor. Likewise pellagra and beri-beri, the Vitamin B deficient diseases, did not have time to establish themselves—not after the restorative powers of Otaheite.

For almost three weeks they had sailed through rain and upon seas whipped up by the wind. It was never so cold that it would kill them quickly the way hypothermia does, but it was constant and compounded by their wet clothes and small rations. The wind dehydrates and the body shivers to keep up what heat it can make for itself, and the harder it works the more it must suck from the nutrition it receives. If the rain saved them from death by thirst it would have eventually killed them through exposure, wearing them down to the point where they became vulnerable to all manner of fevers and chills. And despite their survival so far, some of them were suffering damage which would remain hidden for the moment but subsequently become apparent.

Two years later, Bligh would be given command of the *Providence* and *Assistant* to repeat the *Bounty*'s voyage without the mistakes. The expedition reached the Canary Islands when the fevers and headaches that had begun bothering him before departure erupted with such vigour he was confined to his quarters until the ships were well round the Cape of Good Hope several weeks later. Foaming apoplectically he raged around the cabin, the curses and insults loud enough to rise through the timbers and be heard on the upper deck, before he collapsed into a deep but restless sleep for a couple of days. His crew thought him mad. They weren't to know he was suffering the effects of exposure on the launch in the usual way—a delayed rebellion by his body against the stresses it had endured. The previous year had been spent on land—excepting for his court-martial (a formality) on board the *Royal William* at Spithead. He'd written his account of the mutiny and lobbied the Admiralty to send out a party to hunt Christian and his dogs down, but it took the roll of a ship as it ploughed through the waves, the spray of the water across the bow, the taste of salt and the chill of early Atlantic spring in the air, to trigger memories locked within his organs of just what they'd been put through. His mind may have been clear with the resolve to succeed but his body was frightened and it told him so. Such delayed reactions are common. If, prior to the open boat voyage, Bligh had been a trifle obsessive and too quick with his tongue, from here on fury would cripple him, his body so debilitated it was unwilling any longer to put up with the pressures a perfectionist imposed upon it.

So it was for all of them. As they crossed the Pacific they thought only of the danger of the boat being swamped and the sharks moving in, and of starvation, exposure and scurvy, but a price they would have to pay if they survived was already being calculated. No one then could know the true state of their health, whether pox-ridden, tubercular, or malarial, so the likely physical effects were a mystery. Not to mention how they would stand up to the experience psychologically.

Still the rain came down. It pelted through their sopping clothes, the wool and cotton giving way as the seams rotted and the leather on their belts and shoes split like soggy cardboard. When it had spent itself and was little more than a showery mist the sea life—the boobies and gulls, dolphin-fish and sharks—reappeared, and though the fish swam close enough to touch, no one could get a finger to them and the fishing lines drifted uselessly behind. In despair they watched the clouds return and the creatures vanish.

On the hour, or thereabouts, Bligh took a reading from the sextant. The others looked so sick and haunted he didn't have the heart to ask them to do it any more. He would mark down the figures in their proper place on the page even if it appeared to be but a parchment of unintelligible scrawls to his shivering, delirious mind. If the Great Man's reckoning had been right—and he could assume it was—they were eight to nine days away from the coast of New Holland. Ordinarily that would be just a pleasure cruise for him, but now the distance seemed vast—way beyond anything he could reach with his health intact. For the first time he considered the probability that death would visit before the launch touched solid earth again.

He wasn't afraid for himself, or even for the others. Men of the Georgian Navy were taught they couldn't afford to put too high a value on their own lives. There were others, however, for whom his loss would be inconsolable: Harriet, Mary, Elizabeth, and Betsy, his precious angels.

* * *

SHE LEANS BACK against the velvet settee, a thin, partly nibbled bunch of red grapes dangling above one breast, a small terrier nuzzling the other. She looks a little drunk, lightly amused by the middle-aged painter's boy-like sincerity and sudden bursts of wild-eyed religious enthusiasm, and she plays along with his ideas for poses until, holding the grapes up high above her open mouth as though caught in some Dionysian rite, she goes too far. The joke falls flat. He mumbles something about there being plenty of painters for that sort of stuff down in Cheapside. He, John Russell, carries a royal appointment from George III, and he prefers a more dignified ambience while he works.

As he presses his thumb in to smudge the colours the conversation comes back to that epic voyage. They have spoken of nothing else through the two days of sittings. Once again he tells her it was prayer and redemption that saw those men through. No mortal could have done it on his own wits.

The sun streams through on to Betsy Bligh's chiffon gown, warming her face and increasing her benevolence. She could be sick to the teeth with all the praise people heap upon her husband but, for all his impudence in assuming William needed divine intervention to survive, John Russell is genuinely moved by the story and impressed by the man. Gently fanning herself with a dinner invitation she'd received that morning she thanks him and says how pleased William had been with his portrait . . .

Twelve years earlier, when he sat for Russell, Bligh was just one year back from Hell and still showing the damage. His hands shook uncontrollably, his forehead was damp with a constant sweat, he had poor concentration, he comported himself with the impatient, sometimes bad-tempered, lassitude of the invalid slowly emerging back to health. Russell had disguised all of that and given him the proper poise and dignity a rising lion of the Admiralty deserved. As an added, personal touch, he transported him out of the studio, painting a blue sea, the faint shadow of an island and an Otaheitean canoe in the background. The Empire had just brought most of India and the east coast of New Holland under its domain. It spread now to the four corners of the globe, and there wasn't an inhabited continent without something Britain could call its own. William Bligh exemplified the steady, persistent ambition that made the Empire great—hence the blue sea, the canoe, and Bligh indicating them with his forefinger and a somewhat nonchalant expression. He had pierced the exotic with unswerving courage. Even the most passionate evangelist had to acknowledge that if it had all been God's will, God had chosen well.

Betsy doesn't feel like arguing, but she sees another side to her husband—that strangely sad man obsessively precious about his gifts; fascinating one minute, a sullen bore the next. He has always given the impression he has been victimized, yet he seems wilfully prepared to destroy his career for an insignificant principle. She knows too well there are very few wives of naval officers who can say their marriage, made difficult by long separation, has fidelity, a clear sense of duty, even friendship. She has all three gifts and yet she also has this small but ever present emptiness. His troubles consume him and the most trivial machinations among his fellow officers as they fight for promotion can upset him for days. He is so determined to abide by the letter of the law he can never understand how he aggravates people who know that certain situations require more imagination than he is prepared to put in. They admire him, respect him, call him a hero—but they never warm to him. He has many acquaintances but few, if any, close friends. More than any man she has ever met he feels utterly alone.

His sadness has infected her. Her health is fragile and the rosiness John Russell gives her painted cheeks covers a pallor induced by weeks convalescing in a bedroom with the curtains down. Her complaint is mysterious, but not uncommon among women from the leisured class in eighteenth-century England. Too much sun, too much loud noise, too much excitement bring on dizzy spells. Sometimes she is so weak she can do nothing but lie in total darkness for days on end until she feels her grip on reality fall away. For all she knows, she could have been like this for months—the racket of coach-wheels and clattering horses below her windows beginning to sound as if it is coming from the hall outside the bedroom door.

When she is well she collects art, and shells. None of the artworks is very big. They are mostly prints and engravings, all styles but the best among them by modern scientific artists—botanists and zoologists who have joined expeditions to the South Seas or the Arctic and returned with drawings of the very latest species. She has a taste for *Ancien Regime* France, William Hogarth and comic sporting prints of jockeys and fencers. The collection is large, it is interesting, tasteful and valuable, but it is nothing compared to the shells.

He'd got her interested. He came back from the voyage with Cook carrying a small sack of shells he'd picked up along the way—Van Diemen's Land, the Friendly Isles, Nootka Sound, Kamchatka . . . they had all died, of course, and faded to bone-white, but he could describe the colours they had been, and in the early days of their courtship she listened entranced. Joseph Banks had an enormous bailer shell and some cowries he'd preserved and polished from the *Endeavour* voyage in an enormous display cabinet in his study. He encouraged her with the gift of thirty of them and introduced her to some of the wealthy dilettantes who valued particular shells from the South Seas above all precious gems. Having a husband who sailed into the Pacific three times proved little help at all to the collection. Mostly she found her cowries in the drawing rooms and conservatories of upper-crust

London and Edinburgh, or in tiny shops in the back lanes of seaside towns they were passing through. As the South Seas steadily became more fashionable, anything to do with their natural history took on a whole new value of its own. The real treasures, of course, were the cannibals' terrifying adornments, but sea-shells too had their exotic allure and before long the collection took on professional dimensions. Universities began inquiring about particular specimens and geographical societies asked to have one of their members come and draw them.

None of this intimidated her. She'd grown up in an atmosphere of intellectual passion, surrounded by Scotland's best and brightest minds, she was comfortable even with the brittle etiquette of Navy society. In all things Betsy Betham had impeccable contacts.

In the 1740s the cold, bleak, black-slabbed universities of Glasgow and Edinburgh threw off their heavy, sententious mantles and flowered. Lawyers and historians mostly, the men at the spearhead of the Scottish Enlightenment movement debated the problem of identity subsumed by Great Britain and the suffocating influence of Presbyterianism on the country's wealth. Way too temperate to strike fear in anyone's heart, they were revolutionaries nevertheless—openly atheistic, unfashionably liberal, visionary. Inspired first by the radical French philosophers—Voltaire, Diderot—and by the Englishman John Locke, as their thinking became more focused and the possibilities clearer they began proposing the earliest theories of what would become modern economics and sociology.

As a foretaste, nobody actually understood David Hume's *Treatise on Human Nature*. He published it anonymously in 1740, admitting to a colleague 'it fell dead-born from the press', and the only people prepared to criticize it with any patience were his friends. But the *idea* of the book would catch on. The notion that the most abstract human ideals might be measured scientifically was an underlying motif of the Scottish Enlightenment. Adam Smith, fed up with the way religion pervaded every aspect of Scottish life, considered how wealth could be managed in a rational, disinterested way, with the Public Good as the ultimate ambition. At least he realized money was an essential ingredient, which was a step up from the French with their half-baked pleasantries 'freedom' and 'brotherhood'.

Hume, Smith, Francis Hutcheson, Adam Ferguson became international celebrities. From the 1750s on it was inevitable that Europe was about to undergo some dramatic sea-change in its thinking. 'Public good', 'democracy', 'rationalism' rose out of the discontents of a powerful middle class. At the periphery of the movement, Richard Betham, Elizabeth's father, gave up academic pursuits to become a customs officer on the Isle of Man, but he never lost contact with his old school friends.

When William Bligh came around courting in the spring of 1780 he had no stomach for the theoretical discussions of these now aged and weary dignitaries, but they found him intriguing. He had sailed under Cook—the great hero of the Enlightenment with all its emphasis on knowledge and discovery—and he had a head for mathematics. Cartography and economics shared a common faith in the veracity of numbers. The map-maker trying to calculate longitude with few resources used exactly the same processes as the economist attempting to determine Public Good—or so they told him.

Actually, he was never at a loss for words even when debates turned ludicrously esoteric. He was twenty-six and still possessed some of youth's enthusiasm for things new. A part of him wanted to believe in the impossible. Once he married Betsy and they began a family amidst long hard months of unemployment, and once the conviction that he'd been robbed and betrayed by the officers on the *Resolution* calcified into bitterness, the impossible would become tedious, but in the beginning it energized him.

Richard Betham liked long Sunday lunches spent deliberating over Thomas Paine's *Common Sense* or the latest advancements in science. He was a thoroughly decent and entertaining father-in-law and he thought Bligh a very suitable prospect for his daughter, but he could do very little to alleviate the financial distress she and her new husband were going through. For that Betsy had to call on her mother's brother, Duncan Campbell—who was everything the men of the Enlightenment found repellent in humanity.

He was the entrepreneur behind the convict hulks on the Thames—those stinking, ghostly monuments to the depths of English society. They were his babies. He brought the ships in from the sea-ports, had them refitted and saw they were filled to capacity with Irish folk and other criminals. When it became obvious there simply weren't enough hulks to accommodate every pickpocket and horse thief in Britain, and America wasn't going to take any more, he started cutting his losses and loudly advocated transportation to Botany Bay as the solution to everyone's problem.

His most lucrative interests, however, lay in the West Indies. Sugar, tea, rum, tobacco, slaves—there was room on his ships for all of them, and he needed a young man to captain his ever increasing fleet. His niece's new husband was ideal. Not only did Duncan Campbell save William Bligh from penury and probably divorce, but he introduced him to another man with Caribbean interests—Joseph Banks. When the idea of bringing breadfruit from Otaheite to the slave plantations was first floated, Campbell put forward Bligh's name, pleasing the corpulent old sophisticate Banks no end.

All this mattered to Bligh. He worried about Betsy's failing health, he encouraged her to collect art, he admired her father's friends and he was eternally grateful to Duncan Campbell, but as he struggled across the Pacific later, none of them could give him the will to live so strongly as thoughts of his three daughters. Harriet, Mary and Elizabeth. His heart ached for them, and the little stranger (twins as it turned out—Jane and Frances) Betsy had been carrying when the *Bounty* departed.

In a world as rough, vulgar and dangerous as the Georgian Navy it paid to keep a closed heart. Crewmen turned provocative at the slightest sign of softness in their officers. They wanted to return home themselves, not be at the mercy of some blubbering, sentimental fool. Bligh understood he had to keep his feelings hidden, but Betsy was not just his wife, she was his dear friend, as he expressed in letters full of a frankness and sensitivity extraordinary for a man who rarely saw his family, and then most often when he was unemployed. They were bound, not just by similar backgrounds or a mutual love of knowledge and reason, but by the pleasure their children gave them. 'My little angels' he called them in his letters, and in the years ahead, when artful lawyers and friends of the mutineers succeeded in creating a public portrait of him as a violent sadist, it was a cause for bitter irony that he found his most intense and private joy in the gentle life he created with his daughters.

For now all he had was the thought of them as the seas turned the colour of steel and another night threatened to bring down winds to smash the boat to pieces. The pain of missing his daughters and the fear he might drown without seeing them again was not something he thought he could share with the others. Some of them—John Fryer for example—he knew were married, but no one ever spoke about his family. Whether it was because men didn't talk about such things or because Otaheite had driven memories of home from their minds he couldn't say, but it was a delicate subject and no matter how much he wanted to tell them about his girls he wouldn't have known how to broach it without appearing weak.

What solitude he could find—and it was obtainable, even crammed into a boat with seventeen other men— he devoted to his daughters, turning his face away from the ravaged expressions of the crew to murmur a prayer through barely moving lips. He asked God to make sure the girls remembered him and that his dear little stranger would grow up aware he or she had a father who had done some remarkable things.

One morning, when the sunrise was lost behind a thick blanket of black cloud, after he had doled out a scrap of pork and a spoonful of wine to each man, he hunched over, pulled out the notebook and began writing:

O Lord our heavenly father almighty and everlasting God, who has safely brought us to the beginning of this day; In and through the merits of our blessed Saviour through whom we are taught to ask all things—We thy unworthy Servants prostrate ourselves before thee and humbly ask thee forgiveness of our sins and transgressions . . .

Not being of strong faith he didn't really know how to pray. He knew what to ask for and why, but not how to, so he began with a repetitive and hesitant supplication.

We most devoutly thank thee for our preservation & are truly conscious that only through Divine Mercy we have been saved . . .

God was an enigma. What pleased Him, what opened the door to His heart, was a mystery, and Bligh wrote self-consciously, afraid he might be misunderstood.

Thou hast shewed us wonders of the deep, that we might see how powerfull & gracious a God thou art, how able & ready to help those who trust in thee. Thou hast given us strength & fed us & hast shewn how both Winds & Seas obey thy command, that we may learn even from them to hereafter obey thy holy word and do as thou hast ordered . . .

He wasn't used to begging. He found it distasteful and on reflection wondered what he meant when he declared God had sent down the storms just to vaunt His famous powers.

Almighty goodness that we may be always ready to express a thankfulness not only by our Words, but also by our lives in living more obedient to thy Holy Commandments . . .

That was the closest he could come to making a pledge that if he survived he would devote his life to some higher good. He was not one for empty gestures. The only higher good that mattered to him was his family, and with every word he put down he had them in mind.

Continue O Lord we beseech thee, through the mediation of our blessed Saviour Jesus Christ, this thy goodness towards us,—strengthen my mind & guide our steps—Grant unto us health and strength to continue our Voyage, & so bless our miserable morsel of Bread, that it may be sufficient for our undertaking . . .

It was bombastic, prolix, it sounded like some mis-remembered invocation from the old, decrepit preachers of his youth, but it was sincere—and on the evening of the 24th of May the rain cleared.

For three weeks since leaving Tofoa they had been hounded by storms, they were utterly exhausted, no one had slept a full night since fleeing the island, their clothes had rotted under the stinging force of the rain, they were starved, gaunt and filthy, the pork was spoiling and the bread was damp and mouldy grey. But for once the sea was calm and as the moon cruised through the ink-black, star-filled sky, flying fish skipped across the water's surface pursued by a pair of dolphins.

*

John Fryer watched William Bligh sleeping upright, his head slumped forward and his shoulders squeezed uncomfortably between the bodies on either side. After so many nights of constant, harrowing noise the silence was overwhelming as he steered the boat westwards, his mind feeding itself on resentments he'd bottled up through the storms.

Even with his body twisted up and asleep in the most tortuous position, William Bligh looked to Fryer like a smug, self-satisfied individual. Nothing could dent that surface of confidence in his own authority that he liked to convey. He had more time for questions from the most unskilled crew members than he had for John Fryer's support and advice, and in fact he seemed to see the Master's experience as something of a threat. That was the way Fryer saw it— as if having made the vow to get the men home safely, it was to be his mission and no one else's. Perhaps he thought he had nothing to lose. If he failed, the boat and the crew would disappear, and with them the truth about his failure. If he succeeded, the glory—all of it— would be his. No one would know or care that John Fryer could have done the same thing, that he even tried and was prevented. Nobody would care that he endured all the same miseries and torments as the Captain, and no one would call him a hero.

Fryer's recollections of home were at best vague. He remembered Wells and the pier lined with barnacled fishing smacks, but without sentiment or nostalgia, and he thought of Mary, but he had trouble recalling her face. Actually he had been surprised sometimes at how little she meant to him out here. She was not a reason for living through this ordeal—life's countless hardships had taught him to be pragmatic about love and marriage, as about living and dying. It seemed to him that the moment something started to matter, you lost it. It was better to play safe and take life as it came, rather than give your heart away and wait in futility for its return.

On Otaheite he had found everything a man forced by circumstance into that philosophy could ever hope for. Every way he'd been taught to behave back in England had been turned upside down, and suddenly he was free to indulge himself without fear of suffering the consequences. His mind went back to other nights that were calm and balmy like this one, his hammock stretched out between mast and bulwark, listening to the timbers creak and the water lap the side of the ship as canoes slid up and young women clambered up the ladders and came calling to him.

William Peckover had been sitting inside a hut packing knives, magnifying glasses and other knickknacks for a pig-buying expedition deep into the Otaheitean mountains when four Islanders approached and warned him not to leave the village. A family from the inland had been offended and they'd boasted they'd get their revenge by beating up the trader if he came close. Nothing personal, but he was the crewman they were most likely to meet up there.

Peckover reported back to Bligh and he set about getting to the bottom of the story. He couldn't have been at all surprised to hear the offence involved a woman, or that John Fryer had something to do with it.

The woman—a girl really—had paddled out to the

ship every night for a week to lie with the Master. Ignoring the grunts and groans from the other bodies entangled around the decks, she would come up to him, stroke his forehead and ask in a whisper if he had any more cloth to give her. Reaching under his pillow he'd bring out a small square of white cotton he'd 'found' down in the hold as she let her grass-skirt fall and climbed into the hammock.

One night, with the full moon so bright the upper deck was bathed in soft, bright blue light, he told her to roll over so he could try things another way. She refused, for reasons he couldn't comprehend, so he took back the piece of cloth, saying there'd be no more of that until she did as he wanted. On nights such as this the upper deck could sound like an alley-way full of howling cats. Everybody else was too absorbed in their own activities to pay attention to the argument as the girl grabbed the piece of cotton and John Fryer snatched it back. He couldn't believe people as wanton and promiscuous as the Otaheiteans could actually have strict codes of behaviour, but her refusals were determined. He was equally determined to keep the cloth until she relented. In the end she left him and, sobbing and cursing, slipped down the ropes to her canoe and rowed back to shore.

In little over a week the *Bounty* would sail and Bligh was busy overseeing the loading of the breadfruit plants and supplies of fresh fruit, pigs and goats for the leg to Jamaica. Problems such as the rising antagonism between some of his men and the Islanders bothered him, but after six months of soft living on Otaheite such things were bound to happen. It was high time they hauled anchors. He assumed, naturally, that the problems would disappear once normal life was resumed on the open sea.

When Peckover first came and told him of the Islanders' warnings it was just another episode that could be smoothed over with diplomacy. There had already been incidents. A few times his men had broken tabu and almost started hostilities. Three of them had deserted. The women were starting to fight each other over their rights to the sailors and thefts were increasing. When Bligh discovered Fryer was the source in this little drama he gritted his teeth, closed his eyes and shook his head. The behaviour was so typical, the scenario so likely, he didn't bother investigating too deeply, but wasted a morning in an elaborate display of apology to the woman and her family before Fryer resentfully handed over the piece of cotton.

Bligh was impatient to leave and he could scarcely punish the Master when they both knew that others had got away with a lot worse. The matter was duly noted in the log and dropped. Not by Fryer. He disliked Bligh enough already to have begun a private list of his grievances, and now he could add two more. The Captain had taken sides with the Otaheiteans against one of his own countrymen, and he'd humiliated Fryer by making him apologize. To those men he knew were reluctant to leave Paradise, Fryer put what seemed to him a very pertinent question. Why, in six months of being surrounded by the most beautiful women in the world, had Bligh not shown the slightest bit of interest in anything more physical than a handshake?

Now, in the longboat, as the dark shadow of a shark butted the launch, Fryer repeated the question to himself. You had cause to wonder when a man didn't display the normal desires—and if he was as wilful and as self-absorbed as William Bligh you might ask if there was not something mentally amiss with him. Men were human—that's why they broke under strain and gave in to the passions. If they didn't, were they really strong, or merely sick?

Fryer fished. He wanted one incident, one gesture or slip of the tongue that he could hold against the Captain like a loaded gun. He'd seen him snap enough times to know he was every bit human. After all, they were here indubitably through the Captain's actions. Men didn't mutiny without just cause and through history just cause had been shown time and time again to be the captain of the ship. One small incident was all he needed, so that if they did get back to England and Bligh was hailed as some kind of hero, he, John Fryer, could set the record straight.

How to put it to them? With the sun out, Bligh took the opportunity to look at the bread situation and it confirmed his fears. From what remained that was edible he could stretch out to twenty-nine days' worth—enough to get them to Timor if sailing from here on was easy. But it was possible they might not make it to Timor. None of them really knew the passage through Torres Strait and without proper charts he had to reckon on missing the island and having to sail on for Java. Bad winds could blow them off course. The colony might be under quarantine as often happened in the tropics. There were any number of reasons why they might not make it. Call it excessive diligence, but if he didn't take these things into account they could find themselves in unknown seas, the bread-box empty and no chance whatsoever of surviving. He had to stretch the rations another two weeks just to be safe.

He felt the untidy beard that had sprouted across his face. Beards didn't come easily to him but the faces of some of the others were buried under thick mats of hair which accentuated the hunger and despair in their eyes. They reminded him of the wretched primates imprisoned at the London Zoo and it gave him no small anguish to consider how to introduce the new rations.

They all had their ways of eating their morsels of bread. Some of the men dipped their piece in seawater to give it the illusion of flavour and others kept it in their mouths until it dissolved. He broke his bit into tiny scraps and deliberately ate each one, stretching the ritual out for almost as long as a proper meal might take. Actually, he could have lived off reduced rations without a second thought, and that was a part of his problem. The others lacked his self-control, but he had to retain his compassion for them. Some of them were dying, through no fault of their own, and in different circumstances they'd proved they were tough enough to meet his exacting demands.

* * *

A NODDY THE size of a small pigeon sat on the yardarm of the foresail and swivelled its head in a slow-witted assessment of the figures below. Carefully—as carefully as his weak, shaking body permitted—George Simpson pulled himself up and reached out. Unbelievably, the bird continued swivelling its head until his fingers touched its feathers and he had it in his grasp, passing it down to William Bligh who snapped its neck and began hacking it up with a cutlass.

'*Who shall have this?*'

In the long history of British seamen adrift on the open sea this had developed into a standard practice. One person cut up the food into equal pieces for all and another turned his back. The first person pointed to a piece and called out 'Who shall have this?' and the second replied with a name. By this way they avoided the unpleasant situation of one person repeatedly receiving a larger share or, as in this case where they divided up the entrails and the feet as well, one person having no choice but to take the poorest part.

'Who shall have this?'

The small, bloody scraps were handed out and each man quickly devoured his portion. Parts of the entrails were still warm and they slid down the throat the easiest of all. The thick taste of blood and raw flesh was always unpalatable, even to the most ravenous, but it wasn't long before all that remained of the bird was a crimson stain drying in the sun. Even the bones disappeared, chewed and sucked on until every skerrick of goodness was extracted.

In the late afternoon a booby as big as a duck was caught, cut up and distributed the same way. This time, however, Bligh drained some of the blood into a coconut shell and fed it to David Nelson, Lawrence

LeBogue and Thomas Ledward, they being the sickest among them and most in need of nutrition. Nelson in particular looked to be ready, eager even, to depart this mortal coil.

If William Bligh ever had a confidant it was David Nelson. They had first met on the *Resolution*, when the botanist was the expedition's gardener, and they shared a passion for the new boundaries being set by science. While Nelson went out to discover and catalogue new plants, Bligh sketched them. He was a good artist—not good enough to be a professional but good enough for the gardener to appreciate his work, and in their free time the two men would discuss the natural history of the Pacific, modestly aware they were pioneers. When Joseph Banks selected Nelson as botanist to the *Bounty* voyage, Bligh couldn't have been happier. The prospect of two years at sea with a crew of punks and philistines was daunting, but here was a man he could talk to, whose company he could enjoy and opinions trust.

Brown Booby drawn by a naturalist on the Providence

Nelson became indispensable in ways the Captain couldn't have predicted. Because their mission was to collect and transport breadfruit, a botanist was essential but there could have been few, if any, in all Europe with his experience of the South Seas. The requirements for cultivating, loading and transporting the trees involved subtleties even Banks barely understood, and Nelson took on the responsibility for converting and refitting the ship for the leg to Jamaica. On top of that he shared with Peckover previous experience with the Otaheiteans. A quiet, studious man, not inclined to indulge in the rites of Venus, he never compromised himself in the eyes of either his Captain or the Islanders, and managed to win the respect of the crew. There were plenty of men who could master a ship with Fryer's competence and God knew there were more midshipmen-in-waiting inhabiting England's wealthy manors than the Navy could ever hope to call on, but there was no one so eminently suitable to be the expedition botanist as David Nelson, late of Kew Gardens.

The afternoon the *Bounty* anchored at Matavai Bay he had endeared himself to Bligh in an unforgettable way. A delegation of village headmen and chieftains ceremoniously adorned with boar tusks and flowers and covered with tattoos boarded the ships with gifts of hogs and taro to meet the Captain, equally resplendent in his navy-blue uniform embroidered with gold and brass buttons. Some of them remembered Nelson, Peckover and him from the *Resolution*'s visit some ten years earlier and, while informing them of other ships that had visited in the interim, were anxious to have the story that Cook was dead confirmed.

As always, Bligh treated Cook's death as some unnaturally delicate issue, and stumbled along with his explanations while Peckover and Nelson supported him with the reasonable amount of Otaheitean they could recall. Unfortunately their efforts left the Islanders confused as to whether Cook was dead, alive or somewhere in between, until Nelson found the quick wit to step forth and announce that William Bligh was the Great Man's son. As the Otaheiteans smiled and gestured to make certain they'd heard right, the Captain turned to Nelson and squeezed his shoulder. He'd done well and it wouldn't be forgotten.

Now the botanist sat ashen-faced, bent over and hacking his lungs out, his lips cracked and swollen and his eyes shot with rheum. Taking the shell he sipped the blood, screwing his face up at the warm and repulsive taste before passing it on to LeBogue. His mouth and beard smeared with crimson, he suddenly looked closer to death's door, and Bligh thought back to that moment yesterday when he'd announced there'd be new rations. There'd been little complaint, but then there'd been no actual acceptance. Essentially, the men had been too weak to contest this latest imposition. He couldn't forget Nelson's face, though. As he was giving his reasons the botanist had stared out to sea with incredible venom for a dying man, then spat upon the water. With that gesture his spirit left, and he had turned back to the Captain too sick to fight, too disgusted to complain. Bligh, meanwhile, had refused to confront anyone, and looked away to the distant clouds on the port beam. There seemed little point in trying to convince them he'd not taken the decision lightly, or that he'd taken it because he cared. Hunger had already drained them and if they hated him for his rigour and determination there was precious little anyone could do about it.

A booby foolishly perched on the bow and when they killed it and cut it up they discovered, to their joy, some small flying fish and squid in its stomach. There was enough for each of them to have a piece of fish with their bird-meat and offal, and they took their portions greedily, savouring the slimy and somewhat tasteless squid as if it was some precious, exotic morsel. When they'd eaten they licked the blood off their fingers and settled back. It had barely made a difference nutritionally, but in their famished state it seemed like a feast.

With the moon high and the position of Alpha Centauri close to what he guessed to be midnight, William Peckover reached across a couple of bodies and shook John Fryer awake to take over the helm. The Master had been sleeping soundly since sunset, like the others enervated by the harsh bright sun and the faint breezes that barely ruffled the sails. There had been some cause for high spirits—they'd feasted, so to speak, on raw birds and in the afternoon a tree trunk encrusted with barnacles had drifted past—but with the passing of the storms the sun was about to become their enemy, a hammer pounding the anvil of the ocean's surface. The birds, the tree, and the other detritus indicating land wasn't far away, could not have been more providential.

William Purcell sat beside the Master, the two of them huddled together and whispering as the boat bobbed through the night. Of one thing Fryer was certain. If they got back to England, the first thing he'd do would be to file a complaint against the Captain with the Admiralty. He wouldn't shirk either, for there'd been one death already and any more would leave no one to blame but Bligh. He was starving them to death. The new rations had nothing to do with maybe having to make Java and everything to do with power. The man wasn't *happy* enough to be Captain; he needed to inflict his authority like it was a weapon of torture and the weaker the crew became the more determined he was to punish them. And if they did survive, you could bet your life on who'd be taking the credit. He'd put the record straight, Fryer would. Once his version of events was made public there'd be little wonder there'd been a mutiny. Public sympathy always lay with the victims, and in this situation it would be the Captain's word against that of almost all his crew. Bligh wasn't some innocent brought down by circumstance but a man whose cruelty was calculated.

Purcell agreed. Actually he knew it for a fact. The source of his enmity towards Bligh was forgotten, even by him, but it thrived on a pettiness that made John Fryer appear positively generous and broad-minded. William Bligh had a zealous, even slavish devotion to the rule of law, believing society would collapse without it. William Purcell was utterly amoral. The law offered him, personally, protection, and he'd always made it a point to find out exactly what his rights were and just how much movement they afforded him. If one thing could rouse him from his usual state of apathy, it was someone imposing on his rights.

The night before the mutiny Fletcher Christian had come to Purcell standing on the fo'c'sle and railed bitterly against the Captain. He was at the end of his tether. Bligh had all but declared him a thief and a liar and it was impossible now, after weeks of abuse, to take any more of that. He was set for taking the jolly-boat and making off for Tofoa and he put forward his proposition, fishing for any other takers among the few he knew shared his hostility.

Purcell listened, and calculated. If an Able Seaman or Midshipman mutinied he could always raise the defence the Captain was a brute. If that were true, the sailor still might swing but the Captain risked being de-commissioned and acquiring the ignominy of an appalling reputation. A Warrant Officer like himself, however, had avenues closed to his subordinates. He had the ear of ranked officials in the Admiralty and there were proper processes by which he could make his complaints. If he chose nevertheless to mutiny and was caught, his defence would be perfunctory, to put it mildly. His offence would not merely be against a sadistic Captain but against the Royal Navy itself, and the inevitable reward for that was to have one's head cut off, nailed with a pike and hoisted up for everyone to see. In an oily, serpentine voice he agreed the Captain was a monster but pointed out to Christian that there was precious little he could do about it, being a man in his position.

It was a variation on the same themes present in his dispute with the Captain at Adventure Bay, but this time his life was at stake. Only when he was being herded on to the launch with the other Warrant Officers did he realize he'd outfoxed himself with his own cunning. Now he was out here, half-starved, wracked with cramp in his bowels and joints and barely strong enough to lift a spoon to his mouth. High moral principle had been reduced to a primal, black-hearted loathing.

He assured Fryer that he himself and the Master's brother-in-law, Robert Tinkler, would support any complaints filed against Bligh; likewise George Simpson, Robert Lamb and the two Orkney Islanders, William Elphinston and Peter Linkletter. Seven voices were enough to construct a case against the Captain— and they could be sure others would come to their side before the voyage was out.

The most disturbing accusation Purcell could hold against Bligh was that in dividing up the scraps of food the Captain had held some over for himself. Purcell had watched him so carefully every time the food was shared out there could be no mistake. Perhaps the Captain believed he needed more because the men couldn't make it without him and they needed his strength before their own, or perhaps he was just hell-bent on getting himself home and damn the rest of them, but there could be no mistaking what he'd seen.

Twice Fryer asked him to repeat what he'd just said. 'God knows I'd give my right hand to believe you were lying to me, William.'

'Ask Simpson. He's seen the same.'

The launch skimmed over the water's surface slapped by small whitecaps whipped up by a stiff breeze. Handing the helm to Purcell, Fryer crawled across the others until he reached Tinkler sitting up at the bow. Fryer had weak night vision himself, but he worried that the boy might not be able to interpret the signs of imminent danger unless he was there to guide him. Once he'd squeezed in beside him the two of them could do the job of one.

After some fifteen minutes looking out into the darkness Fryer whispered to Tinkler what Purcell had just alleged against the Captain. Had he seen anything to support the carpenter?

The boy nodded. It could have happened.

'But did it?'

The boy thought again for a moment then nodded his head convincingly. Definitely he'd seen the Captain secrete away a bit more for himself than he'd given anyone else.

Fryer thought about it. He knew he couldn't believe Purcell in the best of circumstances, and the boy would have said he'd seen William Bligh sprout horns if he'd been asked to. So what was to be done with these damning indictments? They were useless unless he could engineer a situation where the Captain was exposed as a thief in front of the whole crew, otherwise he would have to construct something, and that was damn near impossible squashed together on the boat. All threats against Bligh were just that—threats, without substance or any real power behind them.

'You know,' he moved his face close enough that he felt the bristles on his beard touch the boy's ear. 'If you were to see him do anything, or if you heard of something, you'd tell me, wouldn't you?'

Again Tinkler nodded.

'Good lad. Your mother would have my arse if anything happened to you and the Lord knows I'd hand it over willingly if anything did. We're not alone in our opinions of the Captain but we have to tread carefully. We'd look stupid if we laid our charges and everyone else backed off.'

Tinkler agreed. He was not entirely spineless, but he was only seventeen and afraid, and he accepted Fryer's guidance whenever it was offered. He could vouch for George Simpson, having sat beside him for most of the voyage and listened to his complaints, and he promised to work on the others to see if they had the guts to take official action against Bligh.

'The situation as I see it is this,' Fryer began, listing his grievances against the Captain, beginning with Bligh's contempt for his navigation skills, his cowardice and reckless behaviour when they'd been escaping the Feejeean canoes, and the Captain limiting everyone's rations but his own.

Suddenly he froze, squeezing the boy's arm as a request for silence.

'What is it?'

Fryer cocked his ear and craned his neck forward, insisting in a hiss the boy keep quiet. 'Can you hear it?' he called out to Purcell and scrambled up to stand by the mast. 'Don't you hear a noise like the sea roaring against the rocks?'

'Yes, sir, I think I do,' Purcell replied. 'On the quarter.' It was faint and elusive—like a movement in the corner of his eye—but the sound was unmistakable—the distant, regular thump of waves crashing upon reefs.

Then Fryer could see ahead of them the ghostly white of the breakers and cried out to Purcell to port the helm while he lowered the mainsail, dipping it as the others awoke to their shouts and jumped up to assist.

They had arrived at the Barrier Reef.

CHAPTER 4

New Holland

*Two aboriginals of New Holland, advancing to combat
by Sydney Parkinson*

JOHN FRYER TOOK two steps on dry land, swooned and fell flat on his face. The island they had run the launch up on to was low, sandy and sparsely covered with rocks, wiregrass and a few cabbage palms. With the tide out it looked to be an outcrop of the mainland, lying a quarter of a mile away. Not much to speak of, but all the previous day and most of this one they had battled against the currents to find passages through the reefs, and the islands they'd encountered had either proved impossible to land on or turned out to be barren piles of stones. Although it had vegetation, this one appeared to be uninhabited.

Well, not always. The following morning amid the long-cold remains of cooking fires the men discovered the skeleton of an eight-foot snake draped across the dead white branches of a tree—a suitably disturbing welcome for visitors.

The rocks around the shore were thick with oysters, and while Bligh and some men repaired the rudder damaged on a reef the day before, Fryer, Peckover, Cole and Nelson went off to collect enough to stew in the cooking pot. The first full night's sleep since escaping Tofoa had refreshed them, though they were dizzy and weak with hunger, fatigue and constipation, which doubled them over with sharp, short bursts of pain. Being free to walk only made them more light-headed and they were barely aware of the cuts and slices inflicted upon their fingers as they hacked at the oyster shells or tried to prise them open.

Before Fryer and the others had left the main party they'd joined in the general discussion on what was to be done—stay here until everyone was fit enough to travel again, or gather their strength and press on in a hurry. For Bligh there could be no question. The quicker they sailed the sooner they reached Timor, and he wasn't about to abandon his pressing rage at the mutineers. Some of the others, however, thought they'd die if they spent another night on the open sea. When the oyster party left, the discussion had been civil and fairly divided between the two sides. Now, as they struggled up the sand-dunes, they overheard the last part of a remarkable performance.

William Bligh was screaming his head off. In that oddly clipped and efficient accent bred into officers of the Royal Navy he was abusing the men around him with all the vigour of a child denied his sweets. He called them *damned scoundrels* and a pack of ingrates, for it was *his* navigation that had got them here, *his* leadership, *his* skill, *his* determination; and *they* had the nerve to think *they* had the authority to know what was best for them. If not for *him*, *they* would be dead now and this was their way of showing thanks—thinking they could pass over *his* suggestions.

For the benefit of Fryer, Peckover and Cole when they reached the group, David Nelson quietly added the bitter aside that it was also *his* damned economy that had got them into this situation in the first place. A little more generosity and less obsession with expenses and penny-pinching might have seen a more harmonious crew on the *Bounty*. Meaning too that

Bligh's relentless dispensation of such scrappy rations now was killing everyone.

Bligh's tantrum subsided but not before he'd exposed himself to the unsympathetic members of the launch-party. To be sure, each of them had every right to feel themselves come apart at the seams after nearly a month cramped together on that tiny boat, and they had to let off some steam, but for Bligh to jump in before the rest and turn so feral was an invitation to his enemies. He may well have had great navigational skills, he may have been a determined and courageous leader, but he'd also just exposed the flaws in his character, and nobody in Fryer's faction was about to show any sympathy for that. You may as well have asked sharks to ignore the smell of blood.

On this day, 29th of May, in 1660, Charles II had been crowned King and Cromwell's brief English republic formally ended. Seizing on both the pun and the anniversary, Bligh named the island 'Restoration', in honour of a date auspicious to one who held the monarch and English law sacrosanct, and in recognition of the great recuperative powers of dry land. It is a tiny island, marked in only the most thorough atlases, just south of Cape Weymouth and on a parallel with Weipa on the other side of the Cape York Peninsula.

In 1770 Cook had sailed up and mapped the east coast of New Holland in the *Endeavour* and it was the memory of those charts that Bligh now depended on. They were inaccurate, full of gaps, rough guesses and a few wild assumptions. Like the Portuguese, the Spanish and the Dutch who'd tried mapping these waters before, Cook's poor estimations of longitude resulted in distortions to the shape of New Holland that may have mattered had it been more frequently visited. Where he excelled, where he really proved himself as a cartographer, however, was in the charting of the reefs, shallows and small islands littering the northern coastlines. Of course he did. Mapping a new continent might make you famous, but finding the position of a passage through the reefs could save your lives.

Cook's efforts were hampered by the *Endeavour*'s size. It had proved too cumbersome for the intricate passages through the Barrier Reef, and after slow and cautious progress he'd succinctly named these waters the Labyrinth—a maze of hidden traps and dangers. Forced offshore for considerable distances, his charts of the Cape had really been little better than primitive sketches, but of sufficient quality for Bligh now to recognize features on the northern coasts he knew well but had never seen. With a shaky hand but considerable resolve he set about taking readings, sketching coastal views, noting the heights of the landscape visible from the island and estimating the shape of the bays and promontories using the quadrant, the compass and his experienced eye. On one of the small, stained pages of the notebook he drew a map complete with all the major features and landmarks. If anyone ever asked him why, when he was so close to death, he'd persisted with such a chore, he'd shrug and say it was his duty. He was only filling in detail.

Bligh apparently knew nothing of the rumours that

he'd been taking more than his share of the rations. Had he, no doubt it would have created another incident. One thing was certain, however. Someone was stealing the pork. Having assiduously calculated to the half ounce exactly how much each of them could have over a six-week period, Bligh knew he couldn't be mistaken. Pieces of the pork had been surreptitiously cut off.

Reaching dry land had saved them, and within two days each of them felt reinvigorated from the effects, but it also provided a release for the frustrations and animosity built up on the launch. Remarkably, at a moment when they could have been united through their survival, they started going for each others' throats. The Captain approached each of them and demanded to know if they'd stolen the pork. Naturally no one confessed and, especially after that morning's eruption, he was left unsatisfied, suspicious and bad-tempered. With nothing to prove against any of them he decided to fix the problem by chopping up the pork and adding it to the oyster stew. A sensible move, but the seeds of violence had been sown.

The thick clumps of wire grass were a sign that fresh water ran underground, so with the help of several others Bligh began digging. The sand was too soft and collapsed, but a little way down it turned damp. Digging furiously, he soon created a small well from which they could draw up water, albeit muddy with the sand. With the oysters, the pork and some cabbage palm hearts they could boil up a stew which not only satisfied their hunger but provided their first real nutrition in weeks. For a while this small, sparse and rocky island promised them everything they needed, and no wonder some of the men wanted to stay as long as they could. Small wonder too that some of them abandoned common sense and greedily devoured the berries they found on vines growing out of the sand.

Nelson could make an educated guess at the safety of eating some of the berries since they looked similar to edible plants he was familiar with, and—if this was a reliable sign—the birds certainly enjoyed them. Neither he nor Bligh, however, was foolish enough to recommend anything unknown to the crewmen. Still, some of them couldn't help themselves and, thinking they were blackberries or dolichos, crammed the fruit into their mouths.

Predictably they were crippled with stomach cramps. Whether the cramps were the result of toxins or the effect of introducing diuretics to people whose bowels are empty, the men lay bent over and groaning, coming to terms with the cruel possibility that having survived all the Pacific had hurled at them they were about to die miserably from food poisoning.

There was little else to do but watch them and wait to see what course the berries took. In the end they recovered.

The Captain sat in the shade of a cabbage palm making additions to the small prayer book he always carried as part of his kit. The worst was over, he was sure, but he had a duty to express his gratitude and he was mindful that the way ahead was littered with low-lying reefs and atolls, and that sailing by night would be treacherous. Where there was an opportunity, he added in the margins beside the prayer a reference to families, knowing the men who weren't married still had mothers back home who knew nothing of their dreadful circumstances. He asked that whatever happened they might remain in the hearts of the people who loved them and that, should they die, the Lord would take care of their wives and children. His petitions were florid and several times he crossed them out, admitting to himself he didn't know what he'd just written, but as with the prayer he'd composed in the launch, his sincerity was beyond doubt—and it was this he hoped God heard.

John Hallet came up the sandhill carrying a bunch of berries and some water from a rivulet they'd discovered on the other side of the island. Bligh accepted them and watched him walk away, back towards John Fryer who was helping LeBogue mend a sail. The Master stopped him, looked towards the Captain, shrugged and returned to his work.

He'd assumed the Captain was taking readings of the islands around them in preparation for setting sail that afternoon. It surprised him when Hallet explained what Bligh was actually up to.

As noon approached Bligh put down the book, feeling the lassitude brought on by the heat. Below and to his left a crewman waded up to his knees among the coral and the starfish, stooping to gouge oyster shells off the reef with a cutlass. To his right, just a short stroll through the shallows, lay the mainland. He had no desire to cross over and set foot on it. Had there been more time, and had he the force of arms to combat any hostile Indians, he might have considered it a duty for it looked promising. As far as he could see a swath of white dunes protected the inland from the sea, and behind it sat low mountains covered with jungle.

The day before they'd come across two rough bark huts, and someone had found a carved throwing stick, the like of which he'd seen before at Adventure Bay. He knew from the accounts of Cook and others there was some racial or cultural relationship between the people of Adventure Bay and those up here on the north-east of New Holland and that, unlike the Pacific Islanders, they had generally passive reputations, but that didn't make him feel any safer. Whenever Europeans arrived in large numbers and carrying guns, the locals tended to be welcoming. His fear now was that they'd respond exactly as the Tofoans had, as Europeans themselves would once they were aware of the newcomers' weaknesses. It was his strongest argument for staying on the run despite all the obvious benefits of lingering here to recuperate. Another day would not have made that much difference as far as the journey to Timor was concerned—the process of hunting down the mutineers would be slow enough as it was—but if they stayed much longer they could find themselves confronted with several hundred warriors and nothing to defend themselves with but God's will.

By four that afternoon the boat was repaired, the tide was favourable, the water barrels had been refilled, they'd had their fill of stew and they'd dug up enough fern roots to keep them nourished for the time being. Ordinarily he would have argued that sailing through the Labyrinth by night was near suicidal, but so too was waiting around for the inevitable Indian attack.

Satisfied that they were ready to depart, he ordered everyone to the boat, ready to sail. He was pushing off when they heard a loud shout.

Some twenty naked, black warriors carrying spears stood on the mainland, shouting and gesturing to them. Hidden in the dunes behind them they could make out the heads of a lot more, although whether they were women and children or more warriors waiting to attack, Bligh couldn't tell. As it was, they had to sail the launch through a passage between the island and the mainland, although well out of the range of the spears and boomerangs. As they passed through, the cries from the shore became more desperate but, as had happened at Feejee, he could not interpret this. It might be either a plea to come in or something more aggressive. He tacked to the portside, caught the breeze and left them behind. In other times, other circumstances, he might have taken Cook's advice and approached them without fear of violence, but he knew from his experiences at Otaheite he could never traverse barriers with Cook's self-confidence.

Once again Bligh had let go an opportunity to make his mark in the annals of exploration. In the 1790s, if you couldn't discover a new land, the next best thing was to meet its inhabitants. The readers of the hugely popular books of explorers' journals cared nothing for details of shipboard life compared to the exotic thrill of shaking hands with the naked envoys of an unknown race. Everyone he encountered on this voyage, from the old hunchback at Adventure Bay to the warriors at Tofoa, knew of Europeans from having met Cook, and those who hadn't he avoided. William Bligh could not, could never, shake himself free of the Great Man's shadow.

The following morning more natives came down to call them in to shore, one party using the traditional Pacific Islander invitation of waving bunches of leaves, but again he refused to trust their motives. The mainland had changed dramatically overnight. Gone were the high hills and jungle. Now they looked out on low, scrubby dunes and the occasional flourish of mangroves. They were surrounded by tiny islands and through the shallow channels around them flashed schools of brilliantly coloured fish. Bligh ordered the helmsman to take the boat to an island some four miles offshore—a safe enough distance should the locals decide to launch an attack in their canoes.

To the others he appeared to be absorbed in taking readings with his sextant but he was despondent, chewing over certain revelations he'd had at Restoration Island. To begin with there had been his tantrum. He didn't care about that in itself—he was the Captain and it was his right to swear at and insult his crew if he believed they deserved it—but in the process he'd discovered just who among the men he could really depend on: not too many. He'd been shocked. George Simpson, who was so quiet he was just about dead weight on the voyage, had made a comment that proved just which side of the fence he stood on, and even Nelson had thrown him a look about as close to distaste as the old botanist could muster. Then there had been the thieving of the pork. To think someone among them in this their darkest hour could be so selfish, so heartless. God knows he'd seen enough in the Royal Navy never to doubt the capacity for evil in even the most self-effacing individuals, but this was something quite ugly in its mindlessness. What was the thief to do when he'd eaten all the pork and found himself with a few extra days of life ahead of everyone else? If it was the man whom Bligh suspected the fool would have only found himself drifting helplessly, quite unable to escape the stench and the sight of the maggoty corpses—a well-deserved fate if ever there was one.

He brooded. He'd given so much of himself to these men only to have his face slapped, his teeth kicked in and, much worse than that, his authority derided by men who would have been utterly useless without him.

They'd hardly set foot on their next landfall, Sunday Island, when the tension exploded. Some of them—LeBogue, Ledward, Nelson—were so sick they could not have been expected to go foraging for food. They needed to rest in the shade and to have their strength nursed back. That was plain. The problem was a few among the rest thought they deserved the same treatment. William Elphinston for one preferred staying around the boat to working in the sun. He'd cut his fingers to ribbons pulling oysters off the rocks at Restoration Island while others slept in the shade. Surely he was entitled to a rest.

Fryer wouldn't have that. He would have gladly found food for anyone too sick to look after themselves, but he was as exhausted as everybody else and he wasn't going to lift a finger for any malingerers. If the Captain couldn't solve the dilemma, he suggested splitting everyone into three groups and what each group put in the pot they would take out. If Bligh, he added magnanimously, wanted to stay and care for the sick, he would happily share with him.

The tropical sun beating down, William Purcell wandered across the reefs filling an old flour sack with oysters, clams and mussels. More than conscious of what Fryer had suggested, he fully intended to find exactly enough food for himself and his party. Things being as they were, to do more than what was asked of him would only exacerbate an already volatile situation. After half an hour he turned back, wilfully avoiding a crop of oysters clustered to a rock because he already had his share, and crossed the beach towards the launch, half aware John Fryer was not far behind.

Having lain the sick out and cooled their foreheads with sea-water, the Captain took refuge under a bush. The sun seemed to wring him dry of his energy and his head was buzzing with the heat and the flies. As Purcell came towards him he motioned to the copper pot and told him to empty what he'd found in there.

'Not likely,' was the reply. Purcell had done what was asked of him and he'd wait now to see how much the others came back with.

For Bligh it was offence enough to hear the man's voice. To have to listen to what he had said filled him with disgust. Half sick, half inflamed by the heat of the sun, he rose wearily to his feet, shook the sand from his clothes and called William Purcell a scoundrel and an ingrate. 'If I hadn't been with you, you would have all perished by now.'

'Yes, sir,' Purcell replied with poisonous sarcasm. 'If

it hadn't been for you, we should not have been here.'

'You damned scoundrel! What do you mean?'

'I'm not a scoundrel, sir,' the carpenter—who knew exactly how to get under Bligh's skin—retorted with a certain haughtiness. 'I'm as good a man as you in that respect.'

Whether the heat got the better of his temper or his loathing of Purcell finally overcame his common sense, Bligh grabbed at a cutlass. 'Pick one up yourself, Purcell.'

'No, sir. You are my commanding officer.'

'Pick it up!' He swung, the sword flailing limply through the air. He stopped to catch his breath, his mouth quivering, his knees feeling as though they would give way at any second. 'Fight me, you damned reptile!'

Behind him someone laughed. John Fryer came down the sandhill, all of his humour directed contemptuously at Bligh. 'No fighting here. I'll put you both under arrest!'

The Captain turned and levelled the tip of the cutlass at him. 'If you try to touch me I'll cut you down!' There were tears in his eyes. Try as he could he had scarcely enough strength to hold the sword up.

'Sir, this is the wrong time to talk of fighting.' A small audience had gathered and it pleased Fryer to be by reason the leader right now. 'Put it down!'

Small flecks of spittle appeared at the edges of the Captain's mouth and his body trembled. 'How dare you!'

'Cole!' Fryer called the boatswain over. His moment had finally arrived. 'Arrest him!'

William Cole shook his head and didn't move.

'I'll have you know, Mr Fryer, you're preventing me from performing my proper duties. Dare interfere and I'll use my authority. I will kill you!'

Fryer paused. He wasn't game to call the Captain's bluff.

'That *man*!' Bligh spat the word out, 'told me he was as good as I am!'

'No, sir!' Purcell spoke to Fryer with sly, innocent sincerity. 'When he called me a scoundrel I said I was not—but as good a man as he in that respect. And when,' he looked at Bligh, 'you said you had brought us here I said that had it not been for you we should not be here.' Now how could anyone have mistaken his good intent?

As Bligh scanned the faces around him—Simpson, Hallet, Cole, Hayward, Linkletter, Tinkler, Lamb, Samuel, Nelson and Hall—he realized he could not trust any of them to stand by him in a fight. Hurling the cutlass into the sand he muttered a curt, barely audible apology, spun on his heel and strutted off up the sandhills.

Some time later, after the court-martials, the reprieves and publication of the Captain's own account, John Fryer collected the notes he had made, sat down and wrote his version of events. His spelling, his grammar and syntax were all atrocious because, unlike Bligh and the men who had successfully published their adventures with Cook, he was really only semi-literate and he couldn't afford a secretary to iron out the rough patches.

Captain Bligh call'd me a one side and said, Mr Fryer I think that you behaved very improper—I told him I was very sorry for it—at the same time beg to know in what, he said in coming into the Boat and saying that you would put us under arrest . . .

A secretary too might have restrained him from his more intemperate comments. In the end he could never substantiate his allegations that the Captain filched more than his rations, that he was a coward and that he'd fiddled the books, and Bligh's supporters would seize upon his words as inverse proof of the Captain's valour. After all, if a man's enemies are that petty and mean-spirited . . .

But it mattered that he wrote his account. If he hadn't, there would have been only Bligh's version— that of a victim who'd suffered his ordeal with dignity and a level head. Of course he had. The incident with the cutlass didn't receive a mention in Bligh's notebook and the version appearing in his published narrative was considerably edited down from that which appears in the log deposited with the Admiralty.

From the highest point among the dunes Bligh surveyed the mainland and searched for a route they could take through the reefs that afternoon. He felt less secure here on Sunday Island than on Restoration, certain that, if they'd seen them, the Indians would make an approach. There wasn't much inviting about this place anyway. Mostly it was white sand and low scrub, very little shade and even less food.

Half-buried in the sand below lay an old outrigger canoe, long enough to seat twenty men, its prow ornately carved to suggest a fish's head and studded with small, white shells. He'd seen similar craft filled with warriors out in the islands of the Pacific and, not knowing better, assumed it was local, supporting his fears that they could expect an attack. Most probably it came from the Torres Strait.

That evening, as the launch lay anchored just outside a lagoon protected by rocks, he wrote in his log regarding John Fryer: *Notwithstanding he held an ostensible place as the next officer in command, not a person but considered him a mean & ignorant fellow, ever disposed to be troublesome & then ready to beg pardon.*

David Nelson was dying. He couldn't walk without assistance, his sight was failing, his bowels felt as though they were on fire, he was tormented by an unquenchable thirst. He insisted on helping in the gathering of food but collapsed and needed to be carried on the shoulders of Fryer and Peckover— neither of whom had much strength left themselves. To make matters worse, Cole and Purcell had also joined the sick list. Six men now lay stretched out on the sand, moaning and begging for water.

Dabbing the botanist's forehead with wet cloths and tipping spoonfuls of wine down his throat, Bligh tried to find out if he had any ideas what the cause of the illness was. Had they eaten something poisonous? Was it the oysters?

Too weak to speak in more than a hoarse whisper, Nelson told him of what had been happening. It had started back on Restoration Island. Some of the men had come up to him with berries and asked if they were safe to eat. The question was sensible and several times he admitted he didn't know, but then they started making fun of him. Anything they found, they'd run up to him with it and ask—little red berries he'd never seen, clumps of wire grass, a frond of kelp. Foolishly he'd become annoyed, which only encouraged them to produce a decomposed fish washed up on the rocks, seagull feathers, shells—the more inedible the object the better. In his bad temper he had to admit he may well have snapped at someone that yes, certain berries were edible, even though he hadn't had a good look at them. The stew they had made on Sunday Island might very well have poisoned them.

But Nelson had been weak all along. He'd fallen sick quickly on the Pacific crossing and whether it was through age or some hidden medical condition, he'd been the one all along the Captain suspected might not make it. If the berries had indeed been toxic, Bligh should have had a few more casualties on his hands. Once again there was nothing for it but to wait and see how events unfolded.

It was likely they were all suffering chronic exhaustion, their bodies having consumed what small, precious stores of energy remained. Throughout the crossing they'd been stimulated by the terror of a slow and pitiless death on the high seas. It had given them a will they might not have been conscious of but which kept them alive on their meagre resources. The relief of touching dry land also opened their defences, and the sickness that was their due finally arrived. They were giving up.

It terrified Bligh. He'd expected, naturally enough, that reaching land and eating well would revive the men for the final leg. Instead, they looked worse than ever, clutching their bellies, their joints turning black, their skin blistering in the heat, and for once he felt utterly helpless. The encouragement he'd inspired them with on the crossing sounded hollow. The conviction they would soon be safe did not ring true out here on the edge of the great unknown void that was New Holland.

The sun was almost setting when John Fryer woke up. After a morning spent searching for food he'd returned to the boat, found himself a patch of shade and collapsed, sleeping soundly and oblivious to the sand flies swarming about and infecting his skin. For a while he could hardly open his eyes. They felt glued with sleep his mouth was stale from the sickness at the back of his throat. Briefly too he'd been somewhere else—back in England with its green fields and cobblestone villages.

The Captain was nowhere about. Only Robert Lamb and Thomas Hall were awake, bleary-eyed among the bodies curled up under the bushes, so he called to them to fetch a cutlass and come with him to light a fire for the evening stew. Behind the dunes and among thick clumps of grass they found the skeleton of an old tree with branches they could snap off and split with a good kick.

Digging a hollow in the sand, piling in the branches and some dead grass, he took an ember from the fire the Captain had lit that morning and fed it into the middle. The flames took hold at once and suddenly sparks leapt out, catching the brush around them which exploded like old parchment. Thinking quickly, the Master grabbed at whatever bushes lay around the pile, pulling them out by their roots, flinging them on the blaze and managing to stop it from spreading.

His face flushed with the heat, he turned to grin at Hall just as the Captain came trotting up the sand towards them.

He was livid, his voice so choked with rage he had to struggle to wrench the words out. Of all the arrogant, selfish, ignorant, downright dangerous things to do— lighting a fire so that every God-damned Indian for twenty miles around could see it. John Fryer might as well have sent out his calling card and invited them to drop in for a quick kill. Kicking sand over the fire, he gasped for breath and laid one impotent slap across the Master's ear. He'd had it. He'd fought for his crew, he'd risked his life, he'd suffered deprivations for their sake and he'd done more than every single one of them put together to guarantee their safety, only to see everything come apart at the hands of a clod-pated, unteachable oaf who'd done nothing but whinge and sulk while men with far less training but more courage and dignity than he had endured with a spirit he could not have bought for all the tea in China, his soul was so black and empty. What a hateful, abhorrent slug! What a degenerate parasite! What more spineless and irresponsible behaviour did John Fryer have up his sleeve? What more bright ideas did old whey-face want to endanger everyone with?

'Aye,' John Fryer nodded slowly, looking to his right,

then his left. 'A slug and a parasite I might just be, but the only person I see making a disturbance loud enough to wake up the Indians is yourself, Captain Bligh.'

'I will not forget this, Master Fryer. I'll see your name is filth in every ship of the British Navy. I'll see to it you're treated like a leper whenever you choose to step out of whatever hovel you call home!'

When the Captain had left, Fryer laughed and ran up the dune. 'Hullooo!' He waved to the mainland some two or three leagues away. 'We're over here! It's dinner-time you flesh-eating blackamoors!'

Safely hidden behind a ridge of sandhills, Robert Lamb grabbed a booby by the neck and cracked it like a whip. Tearing at the feathers with his fingers, cracking bones as he struggled for the flesh with his teeth, scooping out the warm insides, he savaged the bird until the scarlet carcass lay at his feet in pieces, mostly undevoured. He tried several times to spit the feathers out of his mouth before running down to the water's edge and washing them out, then, unsatisfied, he climbed up to the top of the ridge and lay still, stained hands ready, until another booby came through the wire grass. It was all too easy. The bird paused before waddling over like an innocent puppy. Nine times in all he caught a bird and ripped it apart with desperate pleasure until he was gorged, his body smeared in shining blood as he collapsed into the sand, violently ill.

Close by and unnoticed, Robert Samuel watched in disgust. The butcher was possessed by a quiet, almost methodical frenzy, sucking at the raw flesh and tossing the remains away like some jungle beast, the blood war-paint on his emaciated torso and the hum of the flies a primitive death chant. Unable to take any more, Samuel slid down the sand-dune and ran to tell the Captain.

It was dark when Bligh caught up with Lamb, the half moon casting enough light to make out the scraps of flesh and feathers plastered to his body. This time there were no words—none Bligh could muster up to express his outrage. Instead he grabbed a dead branch lying on the beach and waled into Lamb, striking him across the shoulders, pushing him against a rock and kicking him in the balls. He could feel in himself he lacked the strength to hurt the man—the branch came down across Lamb's back in soft, pathetic thuds—but he persisted, the butcher cowering and crying out once when a jagged piece of wood cut his hand. He kicked him again and it felt as if he'd just sunk his boot into a sack of old papers, so weak was the force of the blow and so debilitated the butcher.

Bligh staggered off and retched. His chest burned and his limbs wobbled like jelly.

How could they do it to him? How could men whose lives he'd saved laugh at him and treat him with such contempt? It maddened him, made him sick to the teeth, yet he knew too he was much too feeble to stand up alone to the taunts. There was no denying now that the launch carried two parties—those who put up with him and those who refused—and he had half a mind to abandon the second lot out here, to fend for themselves against savages and whatever cruelties lay waiting in the reefs. And yet there would be a failure implicit in doing that. He was determined to get each and every one of them to Timor, alive, and if it turned out they all despised him, so be it. He would succeed and their hatred would be the stamp of their failure. A small and distant voice spoke from inside him. It sounded somewhat like Fryer's thick Norfolk accent and it dared him to stake his conscience against theirs. Who cared for moral rectitude if a weaker man could pull off the same feat? What was the achievement in sailing into Timor with a barrel of good rum still unbroached when they could drink it now and feel their physical strength reignite? A better man than William Bligh would have seen common sense and weakened by now. The voice faded away, its disdain still ringing in his ears.

On 3rd of June the dunes and jungles of Cape York fell behind as the surge of the current pulled them out towards the open sea. Bligh had spent a week on the coast of New Holland, charting the shore, the reefs and islands, taking soundings and navigating through tortuous passages. '*The chart I have given,*' he would write in his narrative some months later, '*is by no means mean't to supercede that made by Captain Cook, who had better opportunities than I had, and was in every respect properly provided for surveying . . . Perhaps, by those who shall hereafter navigate these seas, more advantage may be derived from the possession of both our charts, than from either of them singly.*'

Perhaps. He had made one serious error. From his memory of Cook's charts he believed the Prince of

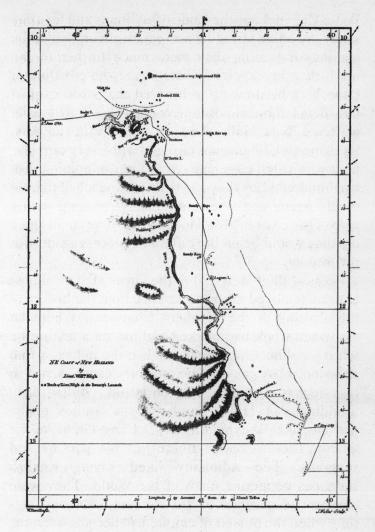

Bligh's map of Cape York

Wales Channel was the Endeavour Straits and for a day sat by the helm, swinging his sextant about, baffled by readings indicating they were much further to the north than he expected. This meant the coastline of Cape York he drew up in his final charts was exquisitely detailed but almost unrecognizable—if that really mattered. New Holland was in constant flux anyway. Its shape and dimensions changed with every cartographer who sailed close enough to form an opinion. For two hundred years they had been getting it half right or totally wrong and when they finally came up with a map of the coast of New Holland everyone could agree on, they would begin the bumbling process again with the interior.

Because Bligh deferred to the Great Man he almost entirely removed his own presence from the history of the charting of the Southern Continent. Where he suspected Cook had marked and named a feature he left it so. Where he thought he had the right to name an island, a bay or a cape he remained cautious, just in case he was intruding. 'Lagoon Island', 'Indian Bay', 'Pudding Pan Hill', 'Sunday Coast'—notes really, nothing like 'Weymouth Bay', 'Cape Grenville' or 'Hardy Isles', Cook's tributes to his patrons and superiors. The Admiralty liked having English surnames peppering maps of the World. They were eloquent testimonies to discovery and conquest at a time when the pursuit of empire had become a frantic, avaricious race between Britain, France and Holland. Had Bligh been more generous with himself, had he seized the opportunity to stamp his presence on the Australian coast, his achievements in map-making and exploring might not have been so quickly forgotten and he wouldn't have wasted years in such bitter defence of his name and reputation.

However, he was later to make an impression on someone. One of the Midshipmen serving on the *Providence* would be Matthew Flinders, who a few years later would circumnavigate and chart the Australian coastline. While the *Providence* sailed through the Great Barrier Reef into the Torres Strait, Bligh spent nineteen days mapping and charting, refining the work he'd done on the voyage of the launch. So good were his charts then that Flinders on the *Investigator* would spend just three days in the area, confident that he did not have to improve on his former Captain's work. Bligh was the link between Cook and Flinders—the two great names in the early cartography of Australia.

Black and yellow sea snakes writhed among the waves about the launch while above it wheeled gannets and boobys. As the islands of the Torres Strait faded from view the sea became choppy and once again they were forced to bale out water. To Bligh it was a minor annoyance. For the first time since leaving Tofoa he felt entitled to relax, confident that however poor their state of health they would make it to Timor. To celebrate, he increased their ration of bread to a twenty-fifth of a pound, three times a day instead of the usual two.

Once again, however, the rough seas chilled them to the bone and after one night knocked about by the waves their maladies returned with a vengeance.

Recuperating had only given them a little more health to be destroyed. Ledward and LeBogue were so ill now there was nothing for it but to lie them out and keep them nourished with the fresh blood from the birds they caught, and the complaints and protests from the rest now had the familiar ring of old songs. Try as he would with his reminders that Timor was just over the horizon, Bligh's encouragement began to sound hollow. Just two days after leaving New Holland he examined their haggard and ravenous eyes and considered what most of them could look forward to if they survived. He had to wonder what point there was fighting for lives that would only ever be a series of constant miseries.

He could wonder the same about himself. The faces of his wife and children that he'd kept vivid in his mind throughout the ordeal were growing fainter, ebbing away like the pulsebeat of a wounded soldier. When he closed his eyes and called them up they were little more than shadows now—ghosts from another life.

Ever since they'd left Tofoa they had thrown over a length of string with an Otaheitean barb tied to it, hoping to catch a fish. As they wound through the reefs of New Holland they had to watch helplessly as schools of cod, snapper and wrasse swarmed past, close enough to touch. Once, at Sunday Island, they'd found a small shark trapped in a tidal pool but apart from that—and what they'd found in the booby's stomach—all their efforts at fishing had been in vain. Now, suddenly, they had a bite and hauled in a young, brightly coloured dolphin-fish. As it flapped about in the bottom of the launch, Bligh clubbed it and cut it up with a cutlass, choosing Samuel to turn his back while he called out, 'Who shall have this?' He could barely contain his excitement as he held the first piece of fish up high in the breeze. Coming fresh after a feast of boobys the night before, it felt as though the good Lord was finally providing for them.

The men gratefully swallowed their portions, scales and all, Bligh receiving a substantial part of the creature's organs. Within hours he felt more vile than he ever had in his life before.

Years later, comfortably seated at a long oak dining table, log fire crackling, a liveried servant slicing at a roasted side of beef, the deep red of the wine reflecting the candle-light, the guests all ears and anticipatory smiles, he might bashfully try to recount episodes from the voyage. The cold that froze his bones, the cramp throbbing in every joint, that constant acidic burn where his wet clothes rubbed against his raw skin. Some pain fades from memory, some doesn't. What he could never forget was the slippery bitterness of the liver of the fish as it slid down his throat, and the violent retching that followed; leaning over the edge of the boat, the water slapping his face as his temples felt ready to explode with every churn in the belly. It was a story he told often—the one that for him expressed all the agonies, the frustration and repressed, seething rage of the boat voyage. He could never understand the nervous silence that followed, but his guests could never understand how someone who'd proven himself so heroically would choose to represent his experience with an incident so insignificant and repulsive.

Now he raised himself up from the side of the boat and stared at the faces floating about him. Even Purcell was concerned. Terrible as all their suffering was, it had been a steady, predictable descent—a shrivelling rather than a collapse. For one of them to start ferociously vomiting suddenly brought their hour of reckoning much closer—tomorrow perhaps, not next week—and that it was the Captain only made it worse. Smiling weakly he wiped his mouth and asked the man next to him to take the helm as the nausea welled up once more . . .

An hour later he took out the heavy leather-bound log he'd kept in the carpenter's box and wrote down the symptoms of the men as he saw them. For most their legs had become swollen, so much so in some cases it produced a morbid bruising he feared could only be cured by amputation, and everybody found themselves slipping in and out of an irresistible yet unsatisfying sleep. At times, as he tried to take readings with the sextant, Bligh would suddenly find himself in possession of an instrument he had no idea how to use. He'd fumble and hope no one noticed, but the blank spots in his mind terrified him. Several times he'd jotted down the latitude and longitude figures for Timor in case he simply forgot, and couldn't find any way back from the abyss of forgetting where the island was.

With the sun setting he took out the prayer book and asked everyone to join him in his petitions. They could barely speak, of course, so the most he was able to extract was a fitful and incoherent mumble, but he was running out of ideas of how to keep them alert. They looked ghastly—cadavers gently nodding themselves to sleep, their joints black and ulcerating, ribs jutting through the flesh cracked like clay from the equatorial sun.

'Really, sir,' William Cole spoke up when Bligh expressed his regret at how terrible everyone looked. 'If you saw yourself you'd think we were doing fine.'

He said it with such innocence the Captain was lost for words, and then, charmed, began to laugh. It was a weak, quite girlish giggle at first, then it seemed to gather strength, almost becoming full-throated and unrestrained before a hacking cough cut it short and he was forced to lean overboard again, retching on an empty stomach.

Around three o'clock on the night of the 12th of June the shapeless silhouette of Timor emerged out of the darkness. They had crossed 6,705 kilometres of open sea, enduring shocking physical conditions—the storms, the hunger, the attack on Tofoa, the despair, sickness, fatigue, the terror—and just a couple more days and they would have started dying. By rights they should have cracked up a long way back, lost their minds beneath a roasting sun, got lost, drifted away, died from starvation and exposure and vanished off the face of the Earth. So this should have been a moment to celebrate the triumph of the human spirit. But what followed was to be a testimony to man's indomitable capacity for bloody-mindedness.

The morning revealed an island of gentle oriental grace, terraced paddy fields spilling down the hillsides, and clearings that appeared to be as sculptured as the finest gardens of Europe. There was nobody about, not so much as a wisp of smoke from a village kitchen, but they could be confident they had left the savagery of the Pacific far behind. Timor was steeped in the fragrance of sandalwood—the smell of opulence itself—and the Dutch colony in Coupang lived in European-designed houses, they went to church, and some of them even spoke English.

The only question was how to get there. No one on the launch knew exactly where Coupang was but Bligh had a feeling that if they followed the coast sou-westwards they'd reach it sooner rather than later. A tropical gale blew in from behind, obscuring the way ahead under a blanket of rain and vapours as they hugged the shore. The island appeared to fall away, then rise again in the distance, and Bligh, fearing they'd become trapped in a bay and unable to ride past the breakers, ordered Fryer to take the helm and make for the open sea while there was a chance.

The Master refused. Anyone with a scrap of seamanship about him could see the distant rise was in fact another island—and anyone who studied the charts as closely as the Captain claimed to ought to know it was Roti.

Bligh shuddered. He could have throttled the man, and laughed while he did it. So close, on the doorstep of salvation, he persisted in contradicting everything as if there was a point to be proved. 'I said, make for the open sea.'

'And I said that's not Timor. That's Roti!' Fryer had to shout to make himself heard above the wind, and the effort nearly broke him. 'I am not spending one minute longer in this damned boat than I have to!'

What offended Bligh, what made the loathing well up so violently inside him, was that John Fryer had only ever done short-haul journeys, he had never set foot in this part of the world until the *Bounty* sailed, and yet he had the temerity to tell a man who had just guided a boat halfway across the Pacific, with something like mechanical precision, that this was Roti—as though he knew it. He was being deliberately provocative and malfeasant, but as usual there wasn't a lot Bligh could do about it. He couldn't slap him, and strong language just bounced off that thick and ignorant hide without making the slightest impression. Once more, and wearily, so he could make a note of the incident in his log and pass it on to the Admiralty: 'You'll do as I say, Mr Fryer. Take the boat out!'

At this point William Peckover spoke up. Unlike either Bligh or Fryer he had been to Timor and knew these waters and the lie of the land as well as could be expected. If his memory served him well it was indeed Roti.

Fryer couldn't contain his small triumph. He knew Bligh had to listen to Peckover, indeed wouldn't dare doubt him, and for one moment of precious conceit he now offered to do exactly as Bligh had ordered and made to swing the helm back and take the boat out.

Bligh himself was not wholly above Fryer's standards of behaviour. When he came to write his version of events he left out the details about the confusion over the two islands. Actually, he claimed all the credit for identifying Roti.

The gale fizzled out and around mid-morning they saw the smoke rising from clearings the natives were making for gardens. Fryer asked the Captain to let Purcell and him get off and search for supplies.

Bligh shook his head. He wanted to reach Coupang, not waste time waiting around for a pair who might or might not be successful.

Fryer pointed to a string suspended above the Captain's head from which they'd dried out oysters found in New Holland. There was none left now, they hadn't caught a bird for several days, and surely there was no point living off old bread and water if they could procure some fruit, even some meat, from the locals?

But the Captain was adamant. Irrespective of the substance of the argument, he was not going to engage in one with John Fryer—and he certainly would not give him the privilege of wandering about for a few hours on dry land while the rest of them waited on the off-chance that Fryer had sufficiently good manners to deal successfully with the locals.

Purcell interjected. The Captain said himself he didn't know where Coupang was exactly. They might be two more days sailing in search of it and in the meantime they'd have to go hungry. That didn't seem right. They'd suffered a lot since being thrown off the ship, and in his opinion they'd shown a lot of courage. They deserved a good meal, even just the opportunity to see if one was around for the taking. One look at the gardens and the palms was enough to tell you these people weren't going to cut their heads off and eat them. There was nothing to lose really, except time, and after so many weeks what were a few hours?

No. Bligh wouldn't hear of it. He was certainly not going to dignify any claims to courage by disputing them and he was not going to make himself look silly letting two wastrels roam about only to discover Coupang was just around the corner. After so many weeks they could wait a few hours.

'Please.' Fryer did not have to try at all any more to look pathetic. 'I'm hungry. We're all hungry. We kept our mouths shut when we sailed past all those islands out in the South Seas. Now I'm begging you, Captain. If we could get just enough to satisfy us,' and he looked deliberately at Lawrence LeBogue's shattered figure in the bottom of the launch, 'it would help.'

The sight of LeBogue, of Ledward and of Nelson could never persuade Bligh that Fryer and Purcell had their interests at heart, but the prospect of reviving them with fresh fruit or vegetables was enough to convince him to let them off. Close enough to the shore, he threw a grapnel out and hauled the boat in.

'So who's coming?' Fryer looked around. 'Mr Linkletter?'

The Quartermaster shook his head. He barely had the strength to sit up straight, let alone go for a walk in the jungle.

'Mr Hall?'

Much the same response.

'Nobody, hey? Well, I'm afraid I'm not getting off. Not with Mr Purcell alone. I'm not risking my neck unless a few more of you come for support.' It occurred to him he might just have provided Bligh with the perfect opportunity to be rid of himself and Purcell.

They had volunteered, and they could find their own way to Coupang. He knew in his heart that abandoning them at Timor would win Bligh a round of applause if the matter ever came before a court-martial.

'It wouldn't be right,' Purcell agreed with Fryer. 'We're not strong enough to do it on our own. We'll find all the food you need, but some of you will have to help us.' He had a voice that could shift from sounding like a paragon of virtue to a martyr without skipping a beat. 'I'm as sick as everyone else but I'm willing to try.'

'Go on, then,' Bligh urged him. 'Get off.'

'I can't risk it, Captain. Not without volunteers.'

All his contempt contained in a flick of the wrist, Bligh jerked the grapnel free and pushed the launch clear. He no longer bothered trying to understand what Fryer's motives were. He'd come to accept the man behaved in a certain way and the best he could do was anticipate it. Soon he'd be rid of him anyway. Once they were off the launch John Fryer could do and say as he pleased.

In the mid-afternoon they sailed into a sandy bay; a thatched hut perched above the rocks, four cows grazing idly nearby and a ratty-looking mongrel sleeping in the doorway. Bligh sent Peckover and Cole up to find the inhabitants and ask directions to Coupang while he completed the notes from his sextant readings. It would be one of the achievements of this voyage that thanks to such diligence people would be able to trace the exact course of the launch, right down to the bay where the inhabitants of the hut came down to meet them.

The men and women all wore cotton loin-cloths and carried steel bush-knives. They kept their hair up in turbans and their teeth were stained a hideous pink from chewing betel nut. They brought down ears of sweet-corn for the Englishmen and pieces of dried turtle, and when they understood that Bligh wanted to go to Coupang one of the men offered to pilot the launch there and hopped in.

He took them through the night, through channels between the islands and past square-rigged fishing boats anchored off the shore. Just before dawn they could make out a small stone fort poking out among the palm trees, the Dutch flag fluttering and the thatched roofs of the town behind it. Coupang.

Picking up one of the small signal flags William Cole used for soundings, Bligh drew a rough Union Jack on it and hoisted it up. He was not one to ignore correct naval procedure and this was, after all, a British vessel.

As they gathered on the beach, a white man surrounded by a group of Timorese called down to them in a perfect English accent from a hill-side. He'd seen the little Jack, he saw the condition of the men and, as his ship was docked at the harbour, he'd take them to meet his Captain, Spikerman. Thinking it wise to keep the launch under guard, or perhaps spotting an opportunity, Bligh decided to appoint someone to the job. 'You,' he ordered John Fryer. 'Stay with the boat.'

As an afterthought he asked John Smith to keep the Master company. Then, with the others, he walked up towards the fort.

CHAPTER 5

Coupang

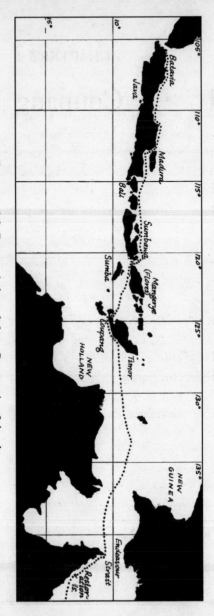

Journey of the Bounty's launch from Restoration Island to Coupang, and of the Resource to Java

WILLIAM ADRIAN VAN ESTE, the Governor of Coupang, raised himself from his death-bed as the tiny Javan servant entered the room with a note on a silver platter. Coupang was an outpost, part of the Dutch line of defence in the fight for control of the Moluccan spice trade. Being appointed Governor could be interpreted as a punishment. Whatever Van Este's offence had been, he'd been sent out to take command of this foetid little colony and fallen victim to a predictable concoction of swamp fevers and malaria. Such was a white man's destiny in those parts.

The servant bowed and backed out of the darkened room, leaving the Governor to consider for himself the hastily scribbled news of some Englishmen arrived in appalling condition. While he read he poured himself a glass of water from the pitcher beside the bed, then he reached across for the silk bell-cord and rang for his valet.

Whatever the state of play between Holland and England—and war was so frequent it was virtually a sporting fixture—it was a matter of protocol, and a pleasure out here in Coupang, to meet another European and a fellow officer, especially one who claimed to have just sailed a launch from Tofoa.

An hour later he sat collapsed in an armchair in the office, his nightshirt dark with sweat and his eyes glazed with fever while he studied the man in front of him. A scruffy beard covered William Bligh's face in patches, his hair was matted, his eyes appeared to have sunk back into his sockets and his skin was cracked by the sun. He was gaunt, the flesh appeared to have withered off his bones, and ulcers and other horrid sores covered his body, particularly his legs. Appearances alone convinced Van Este that this creature had indeed crossed the Pacific, and the miracle was that he had reached Coupang, because he looked literally only moments away from meeting his maker.

Van Este didn't look any better. Hunger and exhaustion had wasted William Bligh, but a close study would have revealed a vigour in the eyes proving there was a lot of life left in him. Not so for the Dutchman. Behind the glaze of fever his eyes were faded and milky, and there was a faint but unmistakable odour of putrescence on his breath. He struggled to listen to the story: an expedition to Otaheite, mutiny, an Indian attack, the storms, the hunger, New Holland, sickness, Timor. The Englishman seemed annoyed at some of his questions but he found it hard to concentrate while the fever steamed away.

As a European in the eighteenth-century East Indies, Van Este had an acute concept of distance. Long sea voyages of any description were an ordeal, and Tofoa was as far away in his imagination as Holland. Even further, for it was somewhere near the centre of that great unknown, the Pacific. He thought about his own condition, the problem of mortality and how it was possible to suffer much worse than swamp fever and survive. The detail that fascinated him the most concerned the rations, and the remarkable claim that having sustained his crew on a scrap of bread and a glass of water for six weeks, William Bligh estimated there were enough supplies to last another eleven days. To a man who ached for the simple pleasures of a sausage and mustard, that sounded unendurable. As he listened he put himself in the boat, going mad with dreams of the vast feasts spread out in an Amsterdam kitchen—the meats, the beers, the soups, the potatoes, cabbage; all luxuries denied to him here.

At last, when the Englishman had answered his final question, he was silent for a while, then exclaimed in a hoarse croak that he had never heard in his life such a remarkable story. All other words failed him. He wanted to express his respect for the courage, the spirit, the resolution and so forth, and he could have without much effort. What he couldn't describe, however, was his admiration for someone who taunted death and survived. That remained ineffable, so he repeated again how remarkable a story it was and asked his son-in-law and secretary, Mr Wanjon, to have a house made ready for his guests and see they had everything they required.

His hospitality was a parting gesture. He would linger about until William Bligh sailed for Batavia then expire.

While John Fryer waited on the beach below Coupang he rummaged through the carpenter's box, found an old blade and shaved himself. It was tough going, not simply because of the thickness of his beard but because the blade was blunt and it had gathered rust through the voyage. There wasn't much else to do—

John Smith, his companion, had a personality to match his name—and after half an hour of concentrated effort Fryer had managed to expose most of his face and cut it up in the process. In his opinion at least he was now the most presentable member of the crew and more dignified in appearance than the Captain.

A little while later a white man came up the beach and presented them with a pot of tea and a basket of cakes, which Fryer and Smith pounced on like dogs and had thoroughly devoured before they found the space in their mouths to say thanks. Thinking the man had been sent down from the barracks, Fryer spoke to him in Dutch, but the stranger replied in English. He was a civilian, he'd heard from some soldiers about the Englishmen arriving, he'd watched Fryer and Smith, and he'd been moved to dig out what remained of the cakes his wife had cooked the day before and bring them down. John Fryer was moved to wipe a small tear from his eye.

When a representative from the barracks did finally arrive, Fryer and Smith had been waiting by the boat some three hours. When they entered the dining room at Captain Spikerman's house they found the rest of the crew sitting around a long table shovelling soup into themselves, a fringe of Dutch officers watching, fascinated by the type of men who could sail a boat all the way from Tofoa on a handful of provisions.

The Dutch expected that the English commanding officer would introduce his second-in-command, but Bligh didn't even look up, obviously ignoring Fryer when he entered the room. Embarrassed, the Dutch officers had to present themselves to the Master, apologizing for leaving him for so long down at the launch.

An outpost, and a charming and motley collection of Malayan, Javan, Dutch and Portuguese architecture, Coupang was also home to a few Chinese, Moluccans and Surabayans. Even Arabs passed through on their trading voyages. For a place of only moderate significance it was remarkably cosmopolitan—the only people who appeared oblivious to the world of international finance were the local Timorese. Bligh sat in the market one morning and watched a man who'd come down from the mountains trade his entire produce of just two potatoes for a handful of betel nuts, and turn back pleased with himself. It was quaint, and he couldn't help thinking of the Otaheiteans with their same commercial simplicity. He even found breadfruit here, among other fruit and plants he'd seen out in the Pacific, and he started collecting specimens.

But Coupang had a malevolent quality too. Bligh might have guessed when he first met Van Este that few foreigners lived long out here. The Pacific was an idyll where only the elderly ever caught disease before the Europeans came, and that was only to hurry up the inevitable. Here in the marketplace a physician could have devoted his life to watching the parade of hideous pathological manifestations.

There was another incident at Coupang which left their Dutch hosts bemused. The colony had run out of chalk and there'd be none until the ships arrived in a few months. Remembering that Purcell had some in his box, Bligh made a gift of it to Captain Spikerman, only to have Purcell confront him the next day with the news that it was his chalk and therefore his to dispense as he wished. Somehow the issue of Bligh sneaking himself extra rations became involved, and before Spikerman had any idea about the true state of relations on board the launch he had the Captain at his door with Purcell and Peter Linkletter under arrest— the latter for supporting Purcell's allegations—and demanding they be taken as prisoners on board his ship. Baffled, Spikerman persuaded Bligh against taking things that far. He could be forgiven for his confusion. The Captain was already submitting reports seeking clemency for some of the mutineers. It appeared that half of the loyalists hated him and half the mutineers had been on his side. Just what *had* happened on the *Bounty*?

David Nelson was the first to die.

Mr Wanjon moved everybody into a large house—a hall, really, with separate rooms for Bligh, Fryer, Nelson and Peckover, and servants in attendance— and while he was seeing to its refitting, Mr Max the local surgeon took care of their injuries and sores. They were celebrities, visited by everyone from the small European community and followed about by the Timorese whenever they found the strength to go out in public.

Once they'd been fed, washed and shaved, given clean clothes and decent beds, most of them made a good recovery. Within a few days Bligh considered himself fit enough to prepare an official report for Mr Van Este, his principle intention being to provide the

Governor with a full list and description of the mutineers, should they ever happen to be passing by. He could remember details about them with frightening clarity: the colour of their eyes, the smallpox scars, the tattoos they'd carved into their skin at Otaheite . . .

He also thought Nelson would like the opportunity to wander about collecting and sketching specimens. Perhaps, but on the one occasion the botanist left his bed he returned drained of all his energy and shivering, despite the tropical heat. Something in his health had been broken irreparably and he could not recover. On the 20th of July he died.

As a tribute, the Dutch arranged an elaborate ceremony, the coffin carried by a guard of twelve soldiers dressed in black, followed by Coupang's European community, the men from the launch, and all the officers from the ships in the harbour. The turnout was huge for a man few of the mourners could claim to have seen. It was in effect a tribute to all the men from the launch, yet throughout the service and through the next weeks Bligh was pensive, distracted while he went about his daily business writing reports and figuring out the best way the rest of them could get back home.

It was a personal blow—not just as a matter of friendship but of history too. Nelson was one of the few from the *Resolution* he'd sustained any affection for, and his death intensified the ineluctable feeling in Bligh that he was returning from the South Seas a failure again. He was not one for discussing his personal anguish with other men, but had he tried he could well imagine the response—disbelief from the

Dutchmen who'd declared his open boat voyage beyond the capabilities of anyone else they'd ever met; scorn and dismay from his own crew, who demanded high standards of inner strength from their Captains. Not even William Peckover—and he'd gone all the way with Captain Cook—realized success meant so much more than simply shipping a whole lot of breadfruit trees to Jamaica. Nelson had known something of this, though. Soon after the funeral, Bligh sat down to write to the one person who might read his letter for the things unsaid, and understand his innermost point of view.

My Dear, Dear Betsy, he began. He wanted her to know exactly what had happened. He was worried he might go the way of Nelson in this decomposing tropical backwater, and he was frightened she'd get news of the mutiny before hearing it from him. That would be heartbreaking. She'd assume he was dead, and, worse, she'd be told he died a scoundrel.

What an emotion does my heart and soul feel that I have once more an opportunity of writing to you and my little angels, and particularly as you have all been so near losing the best of friends, when you would have had no person who regarded you as I do.

He described the mutiny—*Christian holding me . . . with a bayonet at my breast*—the attack at Tofoa and the death of Norton—*a very worthy man*—the crossing to New Holland and the arrival in Timor. *Thus happily ended through the assistance of divine providence without accident a Voyage of the most extraordinary nature that ever happened in the world let it be taken either in its extent, duration, or so much want of the necessities of life.*

Extravagance abated, and he added some personal details. A boy he'd taken under his wing, Tom Ellison, joined the mutineers (and was one of the few to swing for it) and he had some blunt words about John Hallet, whom she had personally recommended for the voyage yet who had turned out to be a worthless slob. Mostly, however, he wanted her to know he had suffered but he'd been brave—*I defied every villain to hurt me.* He'd got out alive, and he'd done no wrong. He was a boy, appealing to her maternal fears and pride—and it was as close as he could get to expressing his greatest desire right now: to have her here, in the room, where he could fall upon her breast and bury his face in it, not just as a man but as a child who needed all of his nightmares purged.

Know then, my own dear Betsy, I have lost the Bounty . . . The letter would become one of the sacred relics of the whole saga, particularly after many of the artifacts were lost or destroyed. When William Bligh had been publicly transformed into a foul-mouthed sadist, his supporters would hold up this letter as evidence to the contrary. Good evidence it was too, except that even to his dear wife he couldn't help himself. His fury against the mutineers singed every word. They were dogs, pirates, cowards and laggards—such atrocious characters that Betsy, as she read the letter, might well have wondered how they found their way on to the *Bounty* in the first place. *It was a circumstance I could not foresee . . . and had they granted me marines . . .* It was all he could offer by way of excuse. Christian and his scumsuckers had not mutinied against his violence or his harsh tongue but against his humanity, and he couldn't give a damn what any court-martial might find against them or even him when they had robbed him of his dreams and ambitions. There could be no recompense for that.

The day after he wrote that compote of heartfelt love and bile he gathered the survivors together to board the *Resource*, a sloop he'd bought on trust down at the harbour, and sailed for Batavia, to catch the October fleet before it left for Europe.

The final showdown with Fryer and Purcell awaited.

CHAPTER 6

Java

TIMOR HAD ITS problems. Java was a hell. Bligh got some idea of what to expect when they anchored off Paffourwang to meet the commandant, Mr Van Rye, and to hire a pilot to take them up to Surabaya. As Bligh rowed through the mangroves to the small fort about a mile upriver, he passed by the carcasses of wild boars scattered about the greasy banks, bloating under the midday sun. Hundreds of them, black clouds of flies rising in a hum whenever his boat strayed close enough. They had come out of the jungle to drink, sank into the mud, and when the tide ran out they were trapped, dying en masse and left there to rot by the Muslim Javans. The stench was disgusting, the atmosphere spectral. For Java, death was a humus on which the island thrived.

Two days later they anchored at the Surabaya road, about a mile off the shore. It was getting dark and too late to row in, and when they woke up in the morning they found three guardboats surrounding them. No strange crews were allowed near the land until they had been given permission, on account of the pirates in these waters.

When he was finally allowed on shore, Bligh was warmly welcomed by the Governor, Mr Barkay, and the Commandant, de Bose. They listened to the story of his voyage across the Pacific with the same mixture of horror and respect as Van Este and likewise were so impressed that they put themselves at his complete disposal. Their one stipulation was that he not sail to Batavia until several other vessels were ready to leave in six days—again on account of the pirates.

William Bligh could not remember another town with such a perfect balance between the civilized and the exotic. Hidden from the coast, except for its flagpole poking above the jungle, Surabaya was surrounded by rice paddies, which the Javans ploughed with buffalo. Across the river from the European settlement was the Chinese town, while the Javans lived in outlying villages shaded by the fringes of the jungle.

On the surface, at least, there was a happy accord, which he attributed in part to the ancient sophistication of the Javans. Most of the far-flung cultures he'd encountered on his voyages were primitive in the absolute. But for their fierce paint or tattoos they went around naked, they used wood or stone, not steel, and belief in a god was difficult to discern except in the grotesque masks and monuments they carved. The Javans wore silks and delicately dyed cottons, their soldiers carried pikestaffs and swords, and they were Muslim. No matter how entrenched the idea of Glorious England and the greatness of things European, he could appreciate that the Javans also had a culture which had obviously percolated through the centuries.

One afternoon Mr Barkay and de Bose took him out to a village whose chief was surrounded by a large and highly disciplined guard. An especially savage tiger had been caught recently and they watched fascinated as the chief tossed one of the scungy village dogs into its pit to be ripped apart.

On the other hand, the villagers were devoted to their buffalo, which they washed and groomed every evening after the work in the fields was over.

Barkay and de Bose took him to another village one afternoon where two chiefs put on a small feast of coffee and rice-cakes while the village gamelan orchestra tapped at their gongs and kettles, plucked at their rebabs and struck the bamboo and steel xylophones. The effect, if a little discordant, washed over him with a graceful hypnosis and he found himself thinking back to another time when he'd heard a more brittle percussiveness—when the Tofoans began beating their stones together and advancing down the beach. In their music as in their lives, the Javans had a structure he might not understand but he could recognize—far removed from the wild passions of the Pacific. He could close his eyes and dream . . .

The next day he returned to the *Resource*. It had been four or five days since he'd seen his crew and happily he'd hardly given them a second thought.

On board, Fryer, Purcell, Peckover, Cole, Hallet, Linkletter and Elphinston were drunk. Their injuries healed, the hunger nourished, the exhaustion driven back with sleep, they found solace in the one thing short of a month's free stay in a local bordello that could relieve what remained of the horror. Sent to the town to pick up supplies, they had bought what they could of the local arrack and called the others to join them on the upper deck, basking in the sun while the liquor gently stewed their minds. So they should have, for while the Captain swanned about the countryside taking in the local arts and cuisine, they had been left to their own devices, awaiting his orders, and for the first time since leaving Otaheite they had the freedom to do as they pleased.

Only Thomas Hayward among the shore party maintained his sobriety, and when word came that the Captain was coming back he tried to get the others on their feet. There were still stores waiting to be collected back on the shore. Thinking back to the Midshipman's tireless passion for work while on the *Bounty*, William Peckover fixed him with a glassy, skeptical eye and wondered aloud what brought on this new attitude. Was it a fever, or did he finally have an opinion of his own, and what's more, one in favour of the Captain?

'Yes,' William Cole slurred, holding the near-empty bottle up to the sunlight. 'Are you *arracky*, or are you a *lackey*?' That seemed, to his own ears, about the funniest thing anybody had ever said, and he fell back on the deck, his whole body silently quivering with giggles while he repeated the joke again and again—in case anyone had missed it.

'What he means is,' Fryer jumped in. 'If the Captain wants his arse licked, Mr Hayward, will you do it? Please do. I'm just a worthless dog and he won't sink that low—not in public anyway.'

Hayward remained unmoved. He could see Bligh coming across the water in a boat with de Bose and the harbour master's attendant, Mr Bonza.

When he boarded, the two Dutchmen turning back, it was plain to Bligh what had been happening. A bottle lay at Cole's feet, Fryer looked pie-eyed and there was a distinct smell of spirits in the air. He said nothing at first but strolled across the deck, let the silence hang as he looked down into the cabin. 'My orders have been disobeyed. You haven't moved those stores.' He picked up a cork that had rolled across the deck. 'Where are Elphinston and Hallet?'

The fact was, they didn't have the others' constitutions and had crawled into the darkness below some time earlier, well and truly smashed.

'Are they drunk or ill or what is the matter with them?'

The question struck Fryer as so disingenuous he couldn't help his own sarcasm. 'Am I a doctor? Ask him what is the matter with them.' He meant Ledward, who looked either deeply embarrassed or half-seas over.

'What do you mean by this insolence?' Bligh spoke so calmly he may have been sincerely interested.

'It is no insolence. You not only use me ill but every man in this vessel and every man will say the same.'

Had he been sober, John Fryer might have been just as intemperate. He couldn't help himself any longer— not since Bligh had treated him so shabbily at Coupang—and if the showdown was to be here and now, so be it. It was inevitable anyway.

William Purcell didn't need encouragement and at once he took the bait, the inebriated smile vanishing from his face as he heaved himself up to confront the Captain. He'd been used ill too, just like everyone else. There wasn't one among them who wasn't sick of the man, who hadn't been starved, heckled and treated like a leper. He'd had enough. They all had. They'd spent six rotten weeks in that boat with him and they were all very sorry they hadn't left him alone and joined the rest in Otaheite.

A bayonet—someone had used it to cut a rope—lay just inside the doorway. Bligh snatched it, swung around and had the tip poking just an inch from the carpenter's throat. He called out to de Bose and Bonza to get back on board, and he advanced on Purcell, pushing him backwards with the point of the blade, the carpenter's throat stretched up. The cold fury in Bligh's voice when he ordered Purcell and Fryer to get themselves below was so measured and hateful, Purcell had no doubt he'd cheerfully run him through. He backed away, towards the door, while Bligh hissed at Fryer to join him. The Master—the same man who minutes before had called Thomas Hayward an arse-licker and a lackey—hesitated just long enough to give the impression he might resist, then he followed Purcell down.

But for those two and the others who were too sick to come up, everyone was ordered upstairs and out on to the deck. He wanted what was to be said to be heard by de Bose and Bonza.

The shore party had gone across to pick up the stores, which had been transported down to the harbour by Mr Barkay's slaves. While waiting they had started drinking until the slaves arrived. Had they been free men there might not have been a dispute, but to the drunken crewmen there seemed no reason why they should have paid four doits for the supplies then had to take them to the boat themselves. That was the slaves' job. They returned to the *Resource* while the stores sat on the docks. The slaves, of course, only followed their master's orders to deliver the stores to the wharf, then went away.

It was humiliating for Bligh to come down to the harbour and see his stores waiting there neglected. It was an affront. Before he could continue his inquiry— in effect his reciprocal disgracing of his whole crew— de Bose called him aside. While they'd been heading back, the cox of their boat had mentioned he'd overheard talk from Bligh's own crew that if he made it back to England he'd be stuffed into a cannon and blown away. Perhaps he was in greater danger than he suspected.

White and shaking, he faced his men and asked if this was true. If so, for the second time on this voyage he had another mutiny on his hands. There was no immediate reply, so at once he asked the Commandant to have everyone personally interrogated.

A better suggestion, in de Bose's opinion, was to ask the cox who he'd heard it from.

'Purcell,' was the reply. 'The carpenter—but the others all agreed with him.'

At this moment Thomas Hayward ran forward and threw himself into the Captain's arms. He couldn't, he shouldn't think that he, Thomas Hayward, had even let the inkling of such a thought cross his mind. He owed the Captain his life and if anyone dared threaten him he would personally stand between whoever they were and his Captain. His shirtfront wet with the man's tears, Bligh found the performance touching. The Dutch thought it odd.

But the threshold had been crossed. The hatred had been made public and Bligh was no longer safe among his own men. He asked if anyone was prepared to make depositions against him and after a considerable silence John Hallet stepped forward, then Cole and Ledward joined him. Bligh ordered them into the Commandant's boat along with Fryer and Purcell, who were to be chained as prisoners.

The following morning Commandant de Bose, his brother, who was a Captain, and Mr Bonza sat on the bench in the courthouse—a small limestone building attached to the local gaol, which was hot and stuffy and barely made more comfortable by the punkah fans operated by an elderly Javan woman. Two marines stood at guard by the doorways and to the left of the judges sat a secretary, preparing his inks. Before them stood William Bligh, dressed in whatever parts of his uniform had been salvaged from the voyage and whatever he'd managed to borrow from his hosts. He sweated and mopped his brow continuously. On some plain wooden chairs to his right sat Hallet, Cole and Ledward. The three of them were hungover and looked miserable in the heat, their eyes bloodshot and their faces pale. They still wore the clothes they'd come off the *Resource* in and they carried the dank smell of sweat and liquor. An earthenware jar of water and some glasses sat on the table in front of them and they sipped frequently. Encountering the Englishmen for the first time, the second de Bose wondered what possible threat they posed to the Captain.

Hallet was called first. De Bose went through the formalities of his name and rank, then asked if he had anything to say against his Captain.

'He beat me once at Otaheite.'

'For what reason?'

'Because I would not get into the boat.'

'Why did you not get into the boat?'

'Because the water was too deep.'

'Have you no other complaint against your Captain?'

'None.'

'Why then did you say to an English sailor now in the service of Holland at this place that it would not go well with your Captain when he returned to England, he having ill-treated every person under his command, for which reason he would be tied to the mouth of a cannon and fired into the air?'

Hallet blushed and glanced at Ledward and Cole. 'I was drunk when I did it.'

Thomas Ledward then took the stand. Once the arrack wore off he'd spent his time in the cells remorsefully, kept up all night by the mosquitoes and the shame of behaving impetuously. He liked Captain Bligh and could not give himself a good reason why he was here, supposedly about to make a statement against his character.

'Have you anything to say against your Captain?'

'I have nothing to say against my Captain.' Then, thinking he *ought* to come up with something: 'Only, the first time the boat went on shore I asked leave to go with him and was refused until he came on board again.'

De Bose raised one eyebrow. That was hardly an indictment. Ledward even looked as though he regretted saying it.

'Have you received your provisions and every other thing allowed you?'

'Yes.'

The Dutchman rolled his eyes at Bligh who rose to examine Ledward. He let the surgeon see the dismay on his face. 'Have I behaved brutally or severely so as to give cause for complaint?'

'No.' A fly buzzed into the room and Ledward followed its path as it came to rest on a window sill.

'Have not I taken every pain to preserve my ship's company?'

'Yes, in a very great degree.'

He then asked Ledward a question that had been asked of Hallet and would be of Cole too. It was on the surface irrelevant to the issue of what had just happened on the *Resource*, but he wanted his Dutch hosts to hear it and he wanted the British people to know it, so he asked his crew to say it. 'Was it possible for me to have retaken the ship or could I have done more than I did?'

'No. Certainly not.'

William Cole was even more contrite.

'Have you anything to say against your Captain?'

He looked straight at Bligh. 'I allege no particular complaint against you, God forbid.'

That part of the inquiry was formally closed—a mere fifteen minutes after it opened. All that remained was for the statements to be signed, everyone to complain about the heat and for the three to be returned to the boat to sleep off their hangovers. No charges were going to come out of this hearing. Once again, however, Bligh had left his hosts wondering what strange relationship he had with his crew. Down in the cells John Fryer tried to play one last hand. He had a letter from Van Este noting the prices of various provisions bought at Coupang, and was now claiming that Bligh had exorbitantly billed these items against the British government. Unamused, Bligh produced all the bills of sale from Coupang to prove otherwise. The Dutchmen gave them a quick glance and said they were satisfied.

Some time later the Master called for another quill and some paper and began writing . . .

Sir

I understand by what the Commandant says that Matters can be settled. I wish to make everything aggreeable as far as lay in my power . . .

He was beaten, his case against Bligh had been blown and he was scared. As he sat in the cold, dark cell he had a vision of the others sailing on home to their heroes' welcome, while he remained here imprisoned by his own passions. Dejected, he knew that to go any further with his attacks would only be an offence against his personal dignity. The Captain would win every hand. His reputation was too secure, he had earned his right to have the final word and he could never be brought down by innuendo alone.

Bligh ignored the letter, ordering that Fryer be placed on one prau and Purcell on another for the trip to Batavia. The court hearing had prevented everyone from sailing under the protection of the Dutch galleons, so de Bose arranged for some heavily armed native praus as an escort. Before they left, Fryer tried again, sending word through de Bose that he wanted to talk. Again he was ignored, but for a letter from Bligh informing him he had no time to communicate.

I beg of you, the Master wrote one more time. *Take me with you if you confine me in irons. I will make every concession that you think proper.*

Such toadying—from a man who had schemed his whole way across the Pacific in an effort to vilify the Captain. It was pathetic, even sad, but he'd shown no remorse when Bligh and the others had really needed it, so now the Captain did write back—informing him he'd make the passage to Batavia in the bottom of a prau, there would be no further communication between them except by writing, and Fryer was to state his apologies and retractions in a letter. Bligh felt no vindication, and certainly no triumph, just a bitterness that the men who would persecute him always proved to be of such weak mettle.

That day they slipped out of Surabaya into seas infested with pirates to make their way to Batavia. These outlaws were a terrifying prospect. They came from Malaya, Borneo, Java and China, and their armies included escaped slaves. They hated the Europeans, plundering their cargo, burning the vessels, laughing as they tossed the bloodied white men to the sharks, but for once Bligh permitted himself the pleasure of relaxing. He had forgotten what life without John Fryer occupying the same space was like and it was remarkably good. Everybody looked happier. The skies were clearer. The islands looked prettier. Even the *Resource* seemed to sail easier.

Batavia loomed out of the grey tropical dawn like some ghostly monument. The Dutch East India Company—spice merchants and a nation unto themselves—had built it on top of swamps a hundred and seventy years earlier and now there were more hospitals and quarantine stations in town than churches or barracks. Between 1730 and 1750 over one million people had been killed by disease, and not since the great plagues at the beginning of the last century did Europeans feel themselves under siege from something so invisible and ubiquitous. Isolating the sick was the only real idea anyone had any more. They carted them off to sanatoriums in the jungle from where they never returned.

An incorrigibly sinister town, ensconced behind thick stone walls bristling with cannon, Batavia suffocated under the relentless equatorial heat. For people who'd been cast out on the open sea amid howling winds and bitter cold, the problem now was to find the air to breathe. It was impossible in the tiny, humid rooms, and outside it was as though your own breath was a precious commodity the town sucked out as soon as you opened your mouth. William Bligh had not been there twelve hours before a fever and splitting headaches struck him down.

Taken to the house of the Surgeon-General—all the hospitals suitable for an officer were, as usual, full—he was given the sharp advice that the only cure for swamp fever was to get out of Batavia. The problem was that ships heading for Europe, like the hospitals, were packed, and there would be no way all of the men could travel together.

He began making plans straight away, arranging for the *Resource* and the launch to be sold—at a loss—and finding a berth on the *Vlydte*, sailing for Middleburgh,

Holland, in ten days. There was only room on board for two more. Being the last of his crew he trusted any longer, Smith and Samuel won the privilege and the others were left to make their own way back.

Six days before Bligh sailed, Thomas Hall suddenly opened his eyes, looked wildly about the white room of the hospital, cried out and died. He'd been ill with fevers since Coupang and he'd been moved to a hospital out in the countryside but he was through anyway. The open boat voyage had shattered his health. Batavia only finished the job off. As with many of his crew, Bligh would have moved mountains to keep him in physical health, yet showed an indifference to his personal life or his character. The Captain didn't even know if Hall had a family who ought to be told of his death.

* * *

ON 17TH MARCH, 1790 a small paragraph appeared in *The Times* announcing that William Bligh, fresh from his remarkable voyage across the Pacific, was expected in London later that afternoon. He had arrived in Portsmouth three days earlier.

When Betsy had said goodbye to him in December of 1787 it was without anticipation. She knew then she wouldn't see him for two years and correspondence would be rare. She hadn't had a letter from him since he left Capetown in the early part of 1788, and it hadn't reached her till months later, but she could never have expected anything more than that. Now as she waited for him to arrive in London, the story of the mutiny and the open boat voyage was only just born, yet already it was developing a preposterous life of its own. For two days she refused to listen to the rumours about her husband's behaviour and the mutiny. The families of Fletcher Christian and the other mutineers were already on the warpath.

When she finally saw him standing in the hallway of the offices of the Admiralty, he was surrounded by other men in blue coats and gold epaulettes, a phalanx protecting him from the insidious gossip already attacking the facts. He had lost weight, his face was lined with weariness, and when he came over to embrace her there was a quiver in his voice and his hands that had nothing to do with the restrained emotion of the moment. In keeping with the high standards of etiquette demanded by the Navy he called for an empty office. Once alone, they hugged without saying a word for about ten seconds before he stepped back. There would be plenty of time to celebrate their reunion later. For now he wanted to give her his version of the story, the only one she would listen to.

Three months later the letter he'd written in Coupang arrived.

But for Bligh's retinue consisting of his clerk and his steward—Samuel and Smith—he'd come back alone. To all appearances he'd made the open boat voyage on his own and alone he'd survived it. Spared any whingeing dissent from Fryer or Purcell, and with no one else to contradict him, he had the stage to himself, and he didn't have to do much to arouse a passionate adulation. The Navy hosted extravagant dinners in his honour, he received standing ovations when Betsy and he arrived at the theatre, and he was even given the honour of an audience with George III, still recuperating from his second episode of madness. He pulled off another remarkable feat: displacing the revolution across the Channel as the most popular conversation piece at dinners. By the time the others returned, the story had been well and truly exhausted—for the time being at least, until the trial of the mutineers some years later, when their families were to attack his reputation with effective savagery.

It wasn't just the endurance of the voyage that so impressed everyone now—by the 1790s, tales of survival on the high seas were numerous enough to have established themselves as a genre of their own. No, it was the fact that he and his crew—although they were themselves something of a detail—had crossed that savage, erotic and mysterious ocean, the Pacific. It brought to mind visions of painted warriors screaming for blood and human flesh roasting over fires—the worst fears of a nation who believed their own brutality had a civilized logic to redeem it. To give even greater resonance to the story in those early months, it was widely felt that Christian and his gang had embraced that same savagery. They had turned their backs on everything from their Captain to their families and on the nation itself, and it was deplorable. Otaheitean lust had corrupted some of England's finest. Bligh on the other hand had done the unthinkable and crossed the unknowable—and he'd done it for the sake of his country. At the same time as the rabble were smashing down the system in France, here was a man—an

English man—who'd stood up to anarchy and beaten it back. For a moment there his courage had no comparison to anyone else's but Cook's.

That was why his narrative was such a hit. The man who was certain he'd been snubbed by Lieutenant King and his cronies wrote a book that outsold all of theirs. It had all the dangers of the high seas, it had mutiny, it had the defiance of death, murderous warriors, and just a hint of what went on when the sun went down; but more than that were the words of a man who, without the slightest shred of pomposity or sentiment, loved his country and all its glorious institutions and had tried his best to preserve its dignity.

It was also why so many of the people who rushed out their own accounts of the mutiny and the open boat voyage inflamed the saga with Protestant rhetoric. It was all there—the noble savage and the fallen angels, the hero who resisted all temptation, and his rite of passage from barbarism to salvation. It was the stuff of Jonah, of Job and his many travails, and in the Baptist halls ministers thumped their pulpits. God was not a papist. William Bligh had just proved that. Around this time the London Missionary Society was having its first meetings in the East End. Before too long it had filled up a boat with zealots, Bibles, trousers and frocks and set out to deliver Otaheite.

In May, just two months after Bligh returned and before he'd even managed to bring out his own account, a strange performance opened at the Royalty, a small theatre out by Goodman's Fields. The evening began with a few saucy sea shanties and a dance piece that set out to prove sailors were irresistible to women, then, with the audience in a suitable mood, the lights dimmed and *The Calamities of Captain Bligh* came to life.

The story began with the *Bounty*, a wooden cut-out, sailing down the Thames. To peals of thunder and flashes of lightning, a group of actors mimed their way into the Pacific. The yellow light from the oil-lamps flickering, they sat down on a beach in Otaheite to watch a troupe in blackface and grass-skirts perform a traditional dance. Their movements were guttural and not at all co-ordinated. They stamped their feet and punched the air and every so often one of them would turn her back to the audience, bend at the waist and rattle her skirts. It was authentic—it was exactly how the producers believed the Otaheiteans danced. Having loaded the breadfruit, the white men set sail. Drumrolls, musket blasts—some of the crew turned out to be ruthless pirates! More thunder and lightning and Captain Bligh and his loyal men found themselves in the open boat wringing their hands and screwing up their faces, still in mime. At a place called Timur they were attacked by a ferocious-looking bunch in blackface who shook paper shields and grimaced as they pulled the strings back on their bows. Lucky to escape, the men managed to make it all the way to Capetown where they were embraced by the governor, the Union Jack was raised and, by way of a finale, everyone was treated to a traditional Hottentot dance. Purists may have observed there was little difference between the stage Otaheiteans and the Hottentots in either their costumes or steps, but most of the audience streamed out into the early summer night satisfied that, even if they'd not actually seen the real thing, it had still been a rare and exotic experience.

William Bligh had galvanized an enormous popular emotion. Not since Cook had anyone had such a grip on the public imagination. People, however, would never be sure how to express it.

Bligh had been lucky to get out of Batavia when he did. By the time he reached England news had come through that Elphinston and Linkletter, the two Orkneymen, had caught fever and died within a day of each other, less than a fortnight after he left. Robert Lamb found a passage on a boat in early 1790 but the traumas of the open boat voyage caught up with him and he was buried at sea somewhere between Batavia and Capetown. Of the nineteen cast off in the launch only twelve would return home. Thomas Ledward caught the *Welfare* back to England via the Pacific. The ship vanished; the only clue to his fate was a story passed about in Hawaii a few generations later by a family claiming to be his descendants.

The Admiralty was so impressed with Bligh that they began drawing up plans for a second attempt at the breadfruit scheme. He'd barely found the time to sink into the pleasures of Betsy and his family before he was on board the *Providence* and heading back to Otaheite. It was something of a tradition in the Royal Navy to recognize someone's achievements by sending them straight back where they'd just come from.

The only other ship they sent out at that time was

the *Pandora* under Edward Edwards and he was no explorer. Sent to hunt down the mutineers, he arrived at Otaheite to find the *Bounty* had vanished. Only fourteen of the twenty-two were caught, Christian not among them. The unfortunate prisoners were locked in a cage up on the deck and when the ship struck a reef and sank, four of them went down with it.

Epilogue

COPENHAGEN, 1801

THE BLASTING OF the cannon shuddered through the whole ship as thick, black fumes belched out of the gunports. High above them a topmast shattered and the ratlines fell to the decks. A crewman appeared through the smoke, his shirtfront soaked red with blood and one arm nothing more than a ragged stump. As another ball smashed into the main rail he stumbled against the capstan and fell not far from the Admiral's feet.

Someone grabbed Nelson and pointed back towards Hyde Parker's ship, the *London*, sitting a league away. Unbelievably, signal flag number thirty-nine—the order to discontinue the action—had been raised. Yet the Danes were on the verge of retreat. After an hour and a half of constant pounding, their defence lines had been broken and they were coming apart.

Nelson raised his telescope to the patch of black leather that covered the empty socket of his right eye. 'I . . . really do not see the signal!'

Hyde Parker—Admiral Hyde Parker—in his sixties and besotted with the eighteen-year-old bride waiting for him back in England, chewed his finger nervously as he waited for Nelson to respond to the flag. His one great fear was that he'd be forced into action and return to his cherub an invalid. He wanted caution exercised.

Still Nelson gave no indication that he'd seen the flag so Parker handed the telescope to his Master and asked him to let him know when they responded to his order.

On another ship, John Fryer fiddled with the focus of his telescope until the *Elephant* and Nelson came into clear view. Then he scanned across, coming to rest on the ship right next to Nelson's, the *Glatton*, and the figure standing on the grating and swinging his sword about as he bellowed his orders. There could be no mistaking him, even obscured by the thick billowing smoke and the flames. Short, pudgy, white as a china plate and strutting about like a rooster directing his brood. It was 1801 now, thirteen years to the month since they'd both been tossed off the *Bounty*. For sure Bligh's hair was greyer, his waistline thicker, but the gestures, the short, severe movements of a man compelled by duty and discipline had not changed. He was excited now, urging his gunners on as the sails above him burst into flames and a mast crashed down into the water. He leaned over to shout an order as a ball struck the *Glatton* and knocked him off the grating but he was up in seconds, shaking the sword with a renewed ferocity. He turned. It appeared he gave the *London* and its signal flag a cursory glance before returning to the action.

The sun had not shone brightly on William Bligh for long. The *Providence* expedition turned out to be a small glory. Breadfruit for slaves proved too expensive and became just another scheme among thousands filed away in someone's drawer. When he returned to England this time, public opinion had shifted. The court-martial of the mutineers had taken place.

Among the few the *Pandora* brought back, Peter

Heywood came from a family with even better connections than the Bethams, and they would not stand idle while their boy was treated like a common criminal. Throughout the trial his uncle, Captain Pasley, sat in the court and nodded to his friends up on the bench, while outside his mother and sister called on their friends among London's journalists and editors. Christian's family too found it distasteful that he should effectively be on trial for mutiny while he could not defend himself. His brother Edward, a professor at Cambridge, was an astute lawyer, persuasive and thoroughly deceitful. Like the Heywoods, he was able to seize on the new tenor of the times—the climate of revolution, of liberty and independence—and chip away at the character of the man who had astonished everyone with his epic boat voyage across the Pacific. Was he so heroic? What exactly *was* the crime of the mutineers but to achieve the dreams of every idealist and reach out for a world far removed from Europe's corruption and decay?

If it was easy to portray Christian and the mutineers as young, love-struck—and maybe misguided—visionaries, it was no more difficult to pervert William Bligh into a violent and abusive sadist. There was no shortage of evidence from the mutineers, and in the end it didn't matter how dubious their testimonies were or what Bligh produced to prove otherwise—something hit a chord. The mud stuck.

And there were more mutinies.

Bligh's crew rebelled on the *Defiance*, and on the *Director* they voted to have him replaced. True, these actions were not directed against him personally. They were both a part of the series of mutinies that spread from Spithead to the Nore during 1797—when sailors asked for their first wage rise in a hundred years—but it didn't help to have him around. By then he was known about the traps as the '*Bounty* Bastard', his presence evoking images of a foul-mouthed tyrant beating his crew senseless on a beach somewhere in the South Seas. People who knew nothing of the circumstances or of the personalities involved assumed that a man with so many uprisings against his name had some serious shortcomings.

His reputation mattered and he was hurt by any allegation that his violence or cruelty was the source of what happened on the *Bounty*, but he was protected by powerful men within the Admiralty, there were still plenty out in the public who believed he was a hero, and he had his own self-assurance that he'd done nothing wrong.

He could live with slander but nothing could save him from the pain his family gave him. Soon after he returned from the South Seas, Betsy gave birth to another daughter, Anne. The little thing was hopelessly retarded and she'd grow up mutely reaching out for his hand, unable to show either her joys or her frustrations except by throwing her body about in a grotesque spasm. Only when he'd come back a second time and she was older could they achieve some semblance of a relationship between father and daughter as he pushed her chair through the parks around their home. Others from their set sent their afflicted children out to hospitals in the country where, fees aside, they need never have anything to do with them again. The Blighs kept Anne at home and let her spend her short life with her sisters.

Then Betsy fell pregnant again and gave birth to twin boys, William and Henry, who died a few hours later.

He could have been contaminated by the fevers at Batavia. It may have had something to do with the *Providence* voyage—he was a physical wreck throughout those two years. All manner of theories were thrown about as to why a man could not perform his duties. Whatever, a happy family now carried the weight of tragedy.

And Betsy . . . more and more she retired to the darkness and seclusion of her room. He couldn't understand it because she didn't have that insipid disposition so many of the ladies affected by nervous complaints had, yet the slightest turn in the weather and she was overcome with fatigue and wouldn't reappear for a week. She maintained her collections of prints and sea-shells, but at times it appeared to him to be a routine, filling in time while she was up and about.

The best doctors couldn't explain it—but then they weren't eager to. Neurasthenia being an indication of a young woman's good breeding, it was wise to keep one's patients guessing—both to keep the source of income flowing and to disguise one's complete ignorance as to what the cause was. Neurasthenia had something to do with a weak liver, the delicacy of the blood, the unique English climate, the horoscope. They gave her tea, salves, brandy, and all the while William Bligh felt the roots of his happiness wither. The family he'd worked so hard to create was falling apart through forces none of them wanted, understood or could do anything about. Its pleasures became more fleeting and precious. Bligh did not succumb to bitterness but he held on more tightly to the values he held dear, and those being order, the law, self-discipline and work, his humour began to fade.

From the safety of the *London*, John Fryer watched the battle with an uncertain regret. It was savage, terrifying, yet Parker had vacillated and because of that Fryer would be denied his part of the honours of victory—overshadowed once more by William Bligh.

Fryer had emerged from the court-martial, if anything, an innocuous figure—neither loyalist nor mutineer—and he'd been spared his own trial when Bligh, for whatever motives, dropped all charges against him and expunged most mentions of his poor behaviour from the narrative. The fate of a man who, despite his best efforts, could not arouse strong passions. Miserable.

Between the mutiny and Copenhagen he had spent years at sea, five at one stretch without touching England, and the son Mary had been carrying when he left for Otaheite grew up and followed his father into the Navy without really knowing him. When the boy was killed in Jamaica in 1804, Fryer would be heartbroken—not openly, but in a way from which he emerged irrevocably older and greyer.

By that stage he had done all a Master could and had been given command of storeships, following the fleet and keeping at a safe distance as it battled Napoleon from the Baltic to the Mediterranean. Only William Bligh had ever expressed any complaints against his work. Hyde Parker, the Earl St Vincent, Sir John Jerves, all powerful figures within the naval establishment, commended him for his skills, his diligence and his good conduct.

He returned from Copenhagen to a life of steadily diminishing returns. Mary died from tertiary syphilis, a too common and much ignored end for the wives of the Georgian Navy. By then his eyesight was failing and he needed others to take down his dictation when he appealed to the Navy Board to be relieved of command. He was all but blind when he retired to Wells in 1812. The descent was swift at first but then it dragged on. He would go into spasms, his memory started to fail him, his speech slurred, in his sleep he was persecuted by horrific visions. His four daughters, who cared for him throughout his last years, protested it was the open boat voyage that ruined his health. Perhaps. On 26th of May, 1817, he died, two years after being bed-ridden and unable to remember who they were.

For now William Bligh wiped the tears from his eyes and tried to peer through the smoke and fumes to the Danish ship foundering ahead of him. Its return fire was all but a gesture and he could see men down in the gunports battling to keep the sea from pouring through as it began to sink. The Danes couldn't sustain a fight much longer, their gunships backing away like timid and bedraggled courtiers. A burning spar crashed on to the deck and the flames licked up a ratline, yet he kept up the methodical barrage. Something usually obscured was coming up to the light. He felt himself elevated for the moment above the grubby, mundane world of professional rivalry and the politics of the Navy. He completely forgot the vilification he'd been subjected to these last years. He was even liberated from the love for his family which with its tragedies and sadness kept him in chains he couldn't help but resent. He was an Officer of the Navy after all, and once given a task duty all but consumed his ego. Lesser souls might wilt but he felt utterly calm and self-possessed. It had something to do with the pleasures of completing a job at hand. Something too intrinsic and profound for mere scapegraces to understand. Who among his enemies understood the nature of his will? As though they themselves cowered before it, the cordon of Danish ships broke apart, and a few minutes later they surrendered.

APPENDIX

The Men on the Boat

IN HIS EFFORTS to bring the mutineers to justice William Bligh provided detailed descriptions of them. Nothing so precise survives of the men on the launch, and only John Fryer has a portrait accounted for, but we can be certain of a couple of things. Like the mutineers, on Otaheite (Tahiti) they engraved their skin with tattoos, and not just local designs but English words and phrases of personal significance. Some of the men had tattoos covering their legs and buttocks, some just a few words on their forearm. Take it for granted too that some of them had smallpox scars and, given the rough and callous ways of the Georgian Navy, a missing digit here and there, the scars from a flogging, and war wounds.

WILLIAM COLE (in his 30s) Boatswain
Came off the *Alecto*, a fireship. These were filled with explosives and cut adrift during battle to blow up among the enemy fleet, so he was used to danger. He wanted to stay on the *Bounty* but he also argued that the 'loyalists' be put in the launch and not one of the smaller boats.

WILLIAM ELPHINSTON (36) Master's Mate
That he was still a Midshipman at thirty-six suggests he wasn't cutting a swathe through the ranks and couldn't have expected to go much further. Some say he was sick before he boarded the *Bounty* but with what we're not sure. He was charged with negligence after he

allowed a buoy to sink. Came from the Orkney Islands.

John Fryer (37) Master
Second in command. The *Bounty* expedition was his last opportunity to get anywhere in the Navy. At least twice he inflamed the Otaheiteans with his ignorance of their culture.

Thomas Hall (40) Cook
He wasn't listed in the official complement. Had two ribs broken on the *Bounty* after a fight with another crewman.

John Hallet (17) Midshipman
The brother of a friend of Bligh's wife Betsy, from a wealthy family. Like Thomas Hayward, he ended up on the launch because Fletcher Christian was fed up with his laziness.

Thomas Hayward (22) Midshipman
Came from a family of ten children, his sister a close friend of Betsy Bligh. A classic case of the Midshipman as 'young gentleman', he failed to see why he should do any manual labour. At the time of the mutiny he was sitting by himself watching a shark circle the ship.

Robert Lamb (23) Butcher
Served with Bligh on the *Britannia*. Was flogged after his cleaver was stolen on Otaheite. At the moment of the mutiny he was one of the very first to join Christian but switched sides when Christian asked who else wanted to go in the boat.

LAWRENCE LEBOGUE (41) Sailmaker
An American, LeBogue also served with Bligh on the *Britannia*. Like most of the crew who were devoted to Bligh he received scant mention in the official documents.

THOMAS LEDWARD (24) Surgeon's Mate
Studied Greek and Latin, and then enrolled in the Royal College of Surgeons. Bligh asked for him to join the crew because he did not trust the surgeon Huggan, a chronic alcoholic.

PETER LINKLETTER (32) Quartermaster
Like his friend Elphinston he was an Orkney Islander. They signed on the same day and are often spoken of in the various narratives as a team (but not an item).

DAVID NELSON (40) Botanist
Appointed by Joseph Banks. A botanist at Kew Gardens and on the *Resolution*. Bligh considered him a friend and most of the crew liked him.

JOHN NORTON (36) Quartermaster
Unmarried. Sole supporter of his aged mother, previously served with Bligh and LeBogue on the *Britannia*. He was large, indeed overweight.

WILLIAM PECKOVER (42) Gunner
One of the more curious figures in the history of the exploration of the Pacific, he sailed on all three of Cook's voyages and reputedly spoke fluent Otaheitean. By the time the *Bounty* anchored in Matavai Bay he had

seen more of the Pacific than anyone else in all history—from Alaska to the Antarctic—yet he isn't much more than a footnote to the sagas of Cook and Bligh. On Otaheite Fryer threatened to beat him up.

WILLIAM PURCELL (38) Carpenter
Senior Warrant Officer and the most persistently difficult man on the *Bounty*. William Purcell was arrested several times throughout the voyage, once on Otaheite when he refused to use his tools to cut a stone for some of the chiefs.

JOHN SAMUEL (26) Clerk
Bligh's personal secretary. At the height of the mutiny other men concerned themselves with matters of life and death but he worried about the Captain's log and his other papers, rescued them and so saved the very items that would help immortalize the saga.

GEORGE SIMPSON (29) Quartermaster's Mate
Quiet, hardworking and unassuming—or so it is supposed since there is very little information about him.

JOHN SMITH (38) Captain's Steward
Also served as second cook. As a rule, men named John Smith don't leave their mark on society. He was no exception.

ROBERT TINKLER (17) Midshipman
John Fryer's brother-in-law. Bligh referred to him as the 'boy', which was unnecessarily patronizing.

Sources

Anon, *An Account of the Mutinous Seizure of the Bounty with the Succeeding Hardship of the Crew to which are Added Secret Anecdotes of the Otaheitan Females*, London, 1792

Bligh, William, *A Voyage to the South Seas*, London, 1792

Bligh, William, *The Log of the Bounty 1787–1789*, Surrey, 1975

Bligh, William, *Bligh's voyage in the Resource; From Coupang to Batavia*, London, 1937

Bligh, William and Fryer, John, *The Voyage of the Bounty's Launch as Related in William Bligh's Despatch to the Admiralty* with *The Journal of John Fryer*, London, 1934

Cook, James, *The Voyages of Captain Cook Round the World: Illustrated with Numerous Engravings on Wood and Steel*, London [exact date unknown]

Ellis, William, *An Authentic Narrative of a Voyage*

Performed by Captain Cook and Captain Clerke in His Majesty's Ships Resolution and Discovery, Amsterdam, 1782

Fryer, John, *The Voyage of the Bounty's Launch, John Fryer's Narrative*, Guildford, 1979

Gamble, Maryann, *John Fryer of the Bounty; Notes on his Career Written by his Daughter Maryann*, London, 1939

Acknowledgements

Thanks to Brigitte, Heidi, Corinne, Ann, Clare and Brian, John and Loma, Dr Russell, Michael Duffy and Gail MacCallum. Karli Van Cleef helped make England great—for a consideration. This book is dedicated to him.